NIGEL & CORONA

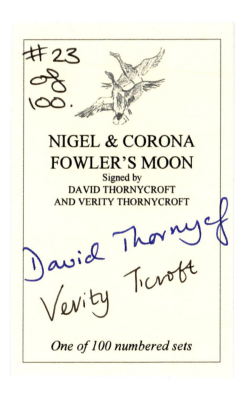

#23 of 100.

NIGEL & CORONA
FOWLER'S MOON
Signed by
DAVID THORNYCROFT
AND VERITY THORNYCROFT

David Thornycroft
Verity Tcroft

One of 100 numbered sets

CORONA THORNYCROFT

NIGEL THORNYCROFT

NIGEL & CORONA

A FAMILY STORY OF ADVENTURE, SPORT, WILDERNESS AND WAR FROM ENGLAND TO AFRICA

DAVID THORNYCROFT

Coch-y-Bonddu Books
2010

Nigel & Corona

Written by David Thornycroft.

Conceptualised & co-researched by Verity Thornycroft.

First published privately, KwaZulu-Natal, 2009.

This edition © Coch-y-Bonddu Books Ltd, 2010
Machynlleth, Powys SY20 8DG.
01654 702837
www.anglebooks.com

ISBN 978 1 904784 26 5

Printed and bound in Great Britain by TJ International Ltd

This book has been compiled from Nigel's book 'Fowler's Moon', his letters and war diaries; Corona's own unpublished memoirs; her sister Rose's diary and memories, and contributions of family and friends, including, in alphabetical order:

David Hamilton, Joe Lubbock, Puss (Patricia) Parkyn, Adrian Thornycroft, Caroline Thornycroft, David Thornycroft, Dillo (Hugh) Thornycroft, Gilly Thornycroft, Guy Thornycroft, Jasper Thornycroft, Jacqueline Thornycroft, Johanna Thornycroft, Justin Thornycroft, Kent Thornycroft, Pamela Thornycroft, Peta Thornycroft, Richard Thornycroft, Verity Thornycroft, and the late Norman Travers.

The illustrations have been taken from Corona's game book, her father Philip's game book, her sister Rose's sketch book and drawings and paintings by all three.

Foreword

The farming community in Wedza, in what was then Southern Rhodesia (now Zimbabwe), was independent, progressive, hard working, and one in which everyone was always ready to help a neighbour in the all too frequent crises inherent in farming in Africa. Within this tight-knit community Nigel and Corona Thornycroft were well known, well liked and widely admired for their robust independence and unfailing standards of courtesy and integrity that some regarded as eccentric. Like the rest of us, they derived their attitudes and standards partly from the way they were brought up and partly from the experiences they subsequently went through, and the aim of this little book is to explain who they were, where they came from and why they were the way they were.

The reason that is important is that they are both now dead and the farm they created, on which their sons grew up, and where their grandchildren knew them, has been stolen by so-called 'war veterans' with Government backing. As their grandchildren and great grandchildren disperse from what is now Zimbabwe to South Africa, Australia, Europe, the Middle East and North and South America, it will become harder for them to remember what Nigel and Corona were like and what made them that way. That would be sad, and it would be worse if the virtues and values they lived by were to be dismissed as out of date or no longer relevant or simply forgotten.

The family asked me to write it because, as the son of Nigel's youngest brother, Guy, I have always been familiar with stories of their shared childhood, and was brought up as nearly in the same way as the second half of the twentieth century allowed. Like Nigel and Corona, I was introduced to field sports at an early age and game shooting has become an abiding passion. Like Nigel and Corona, I keep a game book in which it seemed entirely natural to record the births of my children. Unlike Nigel, I was a professional soldier, coincidentally in one of the Highland Regiments alongside whom he fought in 1940, so I understand something of the nature of his war and captivity. I know less about their life in Africa, although I was lucky enough to visit them several times there, but there are many friends and family who know that part of their lives well and who have been unstintingly generous with their memories.

Their's is a wonderful story and I hope I have done it, and them, justice.

David Thornycroft
North Wales – 2008

Preface to the Second Edition

Chatting with my mother-in-law Corona one day in the late 1980s, I suggested she capture her extraordinary life on paper. Not knowing how to start, I set out for her a simple chronological framework as a working method. Emboldened by this, she began clattering away on her manual typewriter in her two-fingered style and some seven years later, without ceremony, handed over to me several hundred pages of notes.

After her death in 2007, these notes – her memoirs – became, quite suddenly, the inspiration for this book. Her and Nigel's story was there, waiting to be told. My husband, Hugh (also known as Dillo), and my brother-in-law, Richard, backed the idea with generous funds and memories…. and so the journey began. In the 14-month process of compiling this book, across two continents and involving research, interviews, and correspondence, we have missed the voices of the other brothers, Robin, Mike and Pip, but have felt their energies around us.

In January 2010, Corona was acknowledged by the University of Witwatersrand in South Africa for her 30 years of painstaking work to discover and record the San rock paintings of central Zimbabwe with the launch of her collection onto digital archives (www.sarada.co.za). The Corona Thornycroft Collection, housed at the university, recognises her 204 colour paintings and 240 recordings and site notes, as "the primary resource of Zimbabwean rock art".

This, however, is only half the important work she did. Her discovery of a gold burial dated 1450 AD as well as some few hundred further water-colour paintings, site recordings and interpretations are housed in the Harare National Museum, Zimbabwe.

This book was first published privately for the family in hardcover landscape format (some 70 copies) but its reach brought touching messages of remembrance. Fellow countrymen who played cricket with Nigel, painted with Corona, farmed with Pip, shot with Mike and Richard, or who wanted to tell of their own adventures or losses.

I hope this book inspires other families to draw on their collective experiences and to record their own stories.

VERITY THORNYCROFT
BALLITO – 2010

Introduction

This is the story of Corona Gurney and Nigel Thornycroft, a powerful team, their trials and triumphs, a nearly forgotten lifestyle, the adventures associated with their boisterous family and the people who came into it. I was one of them.

I was married to one of the five Thornycroft sons and began visiting Merryhill, with its rolling savannah grasslands and granite kopjies, as a young woman. My Thornycroft memories stretch from early years of marriage and the birth of Nigel and Corona's first grandchildren who adored visiting them at Merryhill. Nigel thrilled his grandchildren with stories about trees and birds and life's accomplishments which he rated: loyalty, the natural world, and decency.

The white-washed huts which were the Thornycroft home when I knew them best, were supremely comfortable and comforting, with roaring fires during the short winter, and bamboos swishing in summer breezes against the roof of the 'new' spare room in the garden which was a regular weekend home for me. Fishing rods, reels, binoculars, tractor spare parts, spanners, were as much part of the everyday décor as the lovely furniture and paintings brought to Africa from England.

Nigel sat writing, usually with a spaniel called Bill flopped onto the uneven floors nearby. He wrote the most compelling and cheerful letters in perfect script, always putting the best light upon what might have depressed others. I only once saw his tall, lean body bowed; he might have even flinched momentarily when he laughed, telling us how Corona had saved him with a shotgun that she used to stop the buffalo which had him on the ground between its legs.

This was a formidable family bonded by love from which grew extraordinary loyalty among the Thornycroft sons. They were each other's best friends as well as brothers.

When I reported Zimbabwe for The Daily Telegraph from 2001 I knew that Merryhill would become a target of land invasions. One Saturday the call came and I rushed out over achingly familiar roads and found Corona at her youngest son's house, on the veranda, sitting straight as a rod and somehow as elegant as usual, bloodied and bruised, with stitches in her forehead. She had just been discharged from hospital after an attack. She was, as always, calm, stoic, and even funny about the assault and her age.

Not long afterwards I dropped in to see her in a retirement village on the outskirts of Marondera, the town closest to Merryhill. Her eyesight had gone, but she still walked miles each day, and she took me into her small flat to show me a photograph of her sons, when they were schoolboys, in cherry red sweaters she had knitted: "Look how handsome they were, how lovely." For all her accomplishments, Corona's focus never strayed from the greatest adventure and love of her life, Nigel and her sons.

PETA THORNYCROFT
JOHANNESBURG - 2010

Peta Thornycroft has reported conflicts in southern Africa for many of the West's leading media organisations over more than 30 years. In 2007 she was mentioned in dispatches for the James Cameron Award in London and was awarded the Life Time Achievement Award for a career of courageous journalism by the International Women's Media Foundation in Washington. She is still reporting.

THORNYCROFT.

GURNEY

CONTENTS

PART I

CHAPTER 1: A HEREFORDSHIRE CHILDHOOD

CHAPTER 2: A NORFOLK CHILDHOOD

CHAPTER 3: GREY GEESE AND SILVER FOXES

CHAPTER 4: NIGEL'S WAR

CHAPTER 5: CORONA'S WAR

PART II

CHAPTER 6: CREATING THE FARM

CHAPTER 7: BRINGING UP THE FAMILY

CHAPTER 8: DOWN THE VALLEY

CHAPTER 9: AT WAR AGAIN

CHAPTER 10: JOURNEYS AND HOMECOMINGS

CHAPTER 1:

A HEREFORDSHIRE CHILDHOOD

Merryhill Wood consists of oak, beech, hazel and holly trees, with bluebells and wood anemones carpeting the ground underneath. It crowns a hill 650 feet above sea level in Herefordshire and was once part of the ancient woodlands of England, so ancient that the lane that skirts it to the North has been worn down by feet and hooves until your shoulders are at ground level in places. It is still a big wood, almost a mile long and half a mile wide, and on a May morning you can hear pigeons cooing and rooks cawing and smell the wild garlic. Later in the year the sounds will be of beaters' sticks tapping purposefully and the alarmed calls of pheasants rocketing towards the Guns waiting lower down the wood.

You look South from the edge of the wood towards the River Wye, invisible but clearly traceable in its wooded banks some two miles away. You can also see the trees that surround Wyecliffe House, but not the house itself. Wyecliffe is four miles as the crow flies but five by road, a long five on a bicycle at the end of a day's sport with the box of ferrets strapped to the pannier and maybe ten or twelve rabbits, gutted and with their hocks neatly spliced, hanging over the handlebars.

Wyecliffe was home to the Thornycroft family from 1910. Before that they lived at Thornycroft Hall in Cheshire, a hundred and twenty miles to the North, passing it from father to son for six hundred years, apart from once, in 1831, when Edward Thornycroft, who would otherwise have been the last of the line, passed it to his friend Charles Mytton, on condition that he and his descendants adopted the name and arms of Thornycroft. That is why nearly all male Thornycrofts today have Mytton as a second or third name.

The Thornycrofts did their duty when called upon. John Thornycroft followed his feudal superior to the Wars of the Roses and was captured at the battle of Blore Heath in 1459. Edward was a Captain of Horse in King Charles' army during the English Civil War. Another Edward was blown up in Spain in 1706 as a Lieutenant Colonel in Sir Charles Hotham's Regiment and is buried in the Cathedral at Alicante. Colonel A W Thorneycroft of Thorneycroft's Mounted Infantry, from a cadet branch of the family, took charge of the shambles on Spion Kop (more properly Spioenkop) in South Africa in 1900. Charles Mytton (Charlie) Thornycroft, Nigel's father, fought in two wars and all four of his sons and his daughter did their bit in the Second World War, two of them giving their lives. But, on the whole, they were content to stay on the land. Thornycroft Hall, with its 712 acres and three tenant farms, was sold when Charlie Thornycroft married. The proceeds enabled his parents to buy a house called Courtlands in Devon and Charlie to buy Wyecliffe House.

Wyecliffe was, and is, an elegant white Regency house, built about 1831, with a gravelled drive and an arched porch, although the family never used the front door. You entered the house from a side door, between a rack for boots of all shapes and sizes and the door to Charlie's study. There were seven bedrooms and three reception rooms, with moulded ceilings, polished oak floors and a fine staircase. It had a courtyard, formed by the stables, the kennels, the coach house and a staff cottage. The grounds amounted to 17 acres, level around the house then sloping down through woods and meadows to the banks of the Wye, with marvellous views beyond to the Black Mountains in Wales.

Charlie Thornycroft was a big man, 6 foot 4 inches tall and heavily built. He served in The Manchester Regiment in the South African War from 1900 to 1902, before resigning to get married. He resumed his commission on the outbreak of the First World War and commanded a Battalion of The Manchester Regiment in France before being invalided back to Britain in 1916. He was a first class shot, a passionate cricketer and a fount of knowledge about birds and animals and the ways of the countryside. He was genial, kind and idolised by his family, although the village postman was in no doubt that he had to be at Wyecliffe House to give the Colonel his post on the stroke of nine before resuming his round wherever he had left it. In 1928 Charlie added a billiard room to Wyecliffe and converted the coach house into a squash court, which is still there, in order to provide outlets for the energies of his four sons and one daughter.

Nigel was the eldest of them, being born on 25th September 1910, almost certainly at his mother's old home, Blawith, at Grange-over-Sands in Lancashire, another substantial house with wonderful gardens, hothouses and greenhouses, all maintained by an army of gardeners. It was built by her father, George William Deakin, and is still adorned with his initials, in stone, in plaster and carved into the wooden panelling, even though it has long since been converted into the comfortable Netherwood Hotel. Nigel spent most of the First World War living there with his grandmother, along with two cousins whom he and his brother Mytton, born in 1912, apparently teased unmercifully. Nigel eventually had three brothers, John (known as Mytton, the family name they all shared), Charles (born in 1915 and always known by his second name of Grey) and Guy (born in 1917), and a younger sister Patricia (born in 1921 and usually known as Puss).

They expended most of their energy out of doors. The boys pursued sparrows with catapults round the outbuildings at Wyecliffe, before progressing onto an air rifle, a weapon that had more killing power when Nigel first owned it than it did by the time it eventually passed to the youngest of his brothers. All round the house were farms and fields in which lived countless rabbits. Evan Rogers, gamekeeper on the neighbouring Brinsop Court estate, of which Merryhill Wood is part, kept count one year because he had a bet that he could kill more rabbits than the 'keeper next door. He accounted for 6,973 rabbits from 1,000 acres in the six months between 3rd October and 25th March. Even then, he lost the bet. They killed over seven thousand on Foxley in the same period. So there were plenty of sporting opportunities. The Thornycroft boys kept ferrets, not least because their father would not allow any of them to fire a gun before his sixteenth birthday. It was a good apprenticeship for a sportsman. Ferrets need constant attention, frequent feeding and much handling if they are to become tame enough to hunt rabbits without line or harness. The purse nets that cover the holes need looking after if they are not to snag or tear at the critical moment. Forays have to be scouted and carefully planned. Much patience and, all too often, hard physical labour with a spade are required if a ferret kills underground since, having eaten, it normally curls up and goes to sleep by the body of its victim. But a successful expedition was the source of great satisfaction, and often a little extra pocket money since rabbits could be sold, both for their meat and for their skins.

When the boys were not ferreting, they canoed on the Wye or collected birds' eggs, then regarded as a legal and healthy occupation, although their father laid down strict rules about the dates after which eggs must not be taken, in order to allow the parent bird a final chance to raise a brood. They learnt to fish for salmon on the River Wye, from which at least one 20 lb fish was taken in their time. Surprisingly, none of the boys took to riding although their father had hunted as a younger, and lighter, man and the stables held a succession of their sister Puss' ponies and horses.

Even when they were not out of doors, they read, or had read to them, books that celebrated the outdoor life and the virtues of independence, self-reliance and physical courage, such as Rudyard Kipling's 'The Jungle Book' and Percy FitzPatrick's 'Jock of the Bushveld'. When the young Nigel was being read stories from 'Wild Animals I Have Known' by Ernest Thompson Seton, all of which, being about real animals, end tragically, he used to listen from behind the sofa in case anything as unmanly as a tear should be drawn from him.

They must also have been swept up in their father's interest in Scouting. Being a very young officer during the South African War (he turned twenty-one while commanding a troop of Mounted Infantry on the veld), he did not move in the same circles as Robert Baden-Powell, promoted Major General for his heroic defence of Mafeking, but he completely understood and approved of Baden-Powell's Scouting for Boys movement, developed from military scouting manuals in 1908. Charlie Thornycroft was actively involved in Scouting for over seventeen years from 1922, when Nigel would have been twelve. He was County Commissioner for Boy Scouts in Herefordshire from 1929 to 1939 and there is a wonderful photograph of him, in shorts and Wellington boots and the wide brimmed hat adopted by the Scout movement, supervising the building of a tree house during a Scout Jamboree at that time.

Once the boys reached sixteen, they were taught to shoot to Charlie's own high standards of accuracy and sportsmanship. For Nigel's twenty-first birthday, in 1931, the family rented Bragleenbeg, a shooting lodge at the head of Loch Scammadale, just south of Oban on the West coast of Scotland, for six weeks. There they were joined by friends and family in relays of half a dozen at a time. Long days spent walking up grouse across the heather would be followed by a duck flight or fishing the evening rise for those who had sufficient energy. When it was too dark to shoot or fish they would return to the lodge for enormous meals followed by games of billiards, bridge, vingt-et-un and others of their own invention. On Sundays and when they wanted a change, they went to Oban and hired the McQueer brothers to take them sea fishing. They were looked after by the staff they brought up from Wyecliffe, consisting of Mr Edgar, the chauffeur, Mrs Dinwoodie, the cook, and five maids, including Janet, the parlour maid, whose starched apron could stand up on its own, and Doris, the house maid, who was so shy that she hid in a cupboard rather than risk being caught giggling with the eleven year old Miss Patricia.

Already employed at Bragleenbeg was a 'keeper, by the name of Clarke, and a pony to carry the game they shot, particularly when they were out after hares, which soon become too heavy a load for a man. He did not have a name, but the pony was quickly adopted by Puss and christened Ginger. By dint of being out all the hours that daylight allowed with rod or gun, sometimes taking both just to see what opportunities offered, they succeeded in breaking every single record for the moor, except for brown trout which they missed by twenty. Their bag for the six weeks was 395 grouse, 18 blackgame, 119 hares, 26 snipe, 17 mallard, 7 pochard, 3 teal, 36 rabbits, 15 curlews, and 9 various. They also caught 27

sea trout, 106 brown trout and 670 sea fish of various kinds. During the holiday, Grey shot his first grouse and his first duck. Guy, being still under sixteen, was not allowed to carry a gun but got his first rabbit with an air rifle and was surreptitiously lent a gun by one of his brothers whenever his father was out of sight. The family rated it the most successful coming of age party that ever was.

In 1940 the Colonel, as Charlie was usually known, took the shooting over Brinsop, of which Merryhill Wood was the first drive of the day and usually the best. Before the war, there had been a pheasant laying pen, a hundred yards long by fifty wide, in Merryhill Wood, from which seventeen hundred pheasant chicks a year were produced. During the war, with most of the farm workers away, Evan Rogers, now head 'keeper, was so busy helping with the farm and keeping the fences in repair that he did no rearing at all, only vermin control. Nevertheless, during the eight years that the Colonel had the shooting, they killed over two thousand eight hundred birds, of which seven hundred were pheasants and the rest mainly grey partridges and wild duck. Quarry recognition had to be precise when shooting duck off the moat round the house as there was a collection of exotic wildfowl, including flamingoes, as depicted in Corona's sketch on page 6. In his memoirs, Evan tells of the morning that he put a covey of eleven grey partridges over a gun line consisting of the Colonel, three of his sons and a friend. There were ten shots and one lone survivor flew on. *"They was wonderful shots"* he reminisced in 1978, still the 'keeper at Brinsop almost forty years later, *"it was lovely to be with gentlemen like it"*. There is a less elevating story that the four brothers were caught poaching and required to show their game licenses at the nearest police station within seven days. Nigel was the only one who had one. He showed it to the police at Cambridge and posted it to Mytton, then at Sandhurst, who posted it on to Grey, at university in Loughborough, and he in turn to Guy, still at Shrewsbury School, all within the seven days and relying heavily on their common initial M for Mytton. It is a record of postal efficiency that the twenty first century Royal Mail could no longer hope to emulate.

The boys played cricket with their father too. All four were tall enough to be useful bowlers and all had the natural athleticism and eye for a ball that made them hard hitting batsmen. The Colonel captained the Gentlemen of Herefordshire cricket team, known as the Hereford Gents, for years and it was not uncommon for the selected eleven to include five Thornycrofts, to the confusion of the hapless scorer. Their mother, Vida, kept a meticulous scrapbook of newspaper cuttings recording all the matches they played in for the Gents, and for their respective schools and universities. It also records tennis and squash matches in which they played with equal, and apparently effortless, success. Mytton played squash for Sandhurst. Grey was Captain of Cricket at Loughborough. Guy played in goal for Shrewsbury School as well as cricket for them and later for his Regiment. Nigel loved his cricket, but affected not to enjoy tennis, which all too often involved girls.

Nigel went to school at Malvern College, to which he was followed by his brother Mytton. The other two boys, Grey and Guy, went to Shrewsbury School. The split perpetuated the conventional pairing by which the two older brothers did most things together, as did the two younger. Puss, who did not go to school at all apart from a finishing school in Devon at the age of seventeen, was left pretty much to her own devices, and her horses.

Nigel does not seem to have had much affection for Malvern, and spent most of the year in which he should have been a prefect, and able to enjoy school properly, in bed with rheumatic fever, allegedly with a catapult and an air rifle for entertainment. However, he did well enough there to win a place at Pembroke College, Cambridge, where he read modern languages. Cambridge did not mean much to him either, apart from his life changing discovery of the East Anglian coast and the sporting opportunities offered by the thousands of ducks and geese that winter there. Indeed, having broken his wrist during his final exams, and despite being awarded several credits towards his BA, he never bothered to return to complete his degree.

Instead, having been turned down by the Sudan Civil Service because of a heart murmur left over from the rheumatic fever, and being completely in thrall to wildfowling, he decided to stay on the East coast and start up a small silver fox fur farm near a village called Blackborough End, between Lynn and Swaffham in Norfolk.

Norfolk was to provide him with his living for the next ten years, the inspiration for the book that made his name, the comrades with whom he was to fight in 1940 and, above all else, probably the only girl in the whole of England whom he would have regarded as a worthy companion on his life's adventure.

BRINSOP   SHOOTING OFF THE MOAT

CHAPTER 2:
A NORFOLK CHILDHOOD

WELREY.

Like the Thornycrofts, the Gurneys were a Norman family and benefited from the parcelling out of England after the Norman Conquest. But while the Thornycrofts seemed content to stay on the land, the Gurneys were more ambitious. Their land was in and around Norwich, by the sixteenth century the second city of England after London. They became wool merchants and subsequently invested in weaving, on which Norwich's prosperity was based. They joined the Society of Friends, or Quakers, well before it was legal or safe to do so, one John Gurney being imprisoned for his beliefs in 1683. Another John Gurney was known as the weaver's advocate for his spirited, and successful, fight against imported cotton and calico in 1720. Yet another John introduced hand spun yarn from Ireland to Norwich and became a Freeman of the City in 1738.

Elizabeth Fry, the prison reformer after whom more girls' school dormitories in England are probably named than anyone else except Florence Nightingale, was born a Gurney and a Quaker. As Quakers, they were accounted sincere and trustworthy and when they founded Gurney's Bank in 1770, it prospered. During a run on the Bank in 1809, caused by rumours of imminent invasion by Napoleon, two friends of the family, both reputed to be hell-for-leather riders and armed with pistols to deter highwaymen, made the hundred mile trip to London several times to collect enough gold to maintain confidence in the Bank. A hundred years later, the family was immortalised in song in Gilbert and Sullivan's opera 'Trial by Jury', in which the Judge kick-starts his career by marrying a rich attorney's elderly, ugly daughter until:

"At length I became as rich as the Gurneys,
An incubus then I thought her..."

One branch of the family expanded into a joint stock company, Overend, Gurney and Company, which was for forty years the greatest discounting house in the world, until crashing spectacularly in 1866. But the original Gurney's Bank in Norwich survived unaffected until it merged with several other banks controlled by Quaker families in 1896 to form what is now Barclay's Bank. Daniel Gurney, who rebuilt North Runcton Hall with no less than forty three rooms in 1835, was a Director of the Bank, as was his son Sir Somerville Gurney, Corona's grandfather, to whom the house passed.

Corona's father, Philip Gurney, was Somerville's fourth son, which meant he was never likely to inherit Runcton Hall. In fact, Lilian Mason's parents, who lived in the even roomier Necton Hall, felt that he was not a good enough catch for their daughter and the couple had to display considerable determination to be allowed to marry, meeting halfway between their two houses at Bauld Bridge, known to the family as the Bridge of Sighs, to which Lilian would drive her pony and trap and Philip would ride. They seem to have been a formidable family, the Masons of Necton Hall. Corona and her sister Rose remembered their father's family home at Runcton with great affection, recalling the stone gateway, the avenue of pollard lime trees leading to the house, and above all the music room, in which stood a piano, a harp and an organ that their grandfather played with exuberant skill. Corona described the house as magical and remembered the butler, Hargreaves, having to leave the dining room rather than disgrace himself by bursting out laughing at the fun and wit flowing round the table.

Necton Hall was a complete contrast, at least in the memory of both girls, although it is only fair to record that their cousin Joe Lubbock, who was brought up there, found it a very happy house. Instead of

Runcton's warm wooden panelling, there were printed notices in the hall commanding you to wipe your feet. Instead of cheerful red walls hung with sporting pictures, there were long stone passages carpeted with coconut matting. There was an organ, in the Chapel where her grandfather read morning prayers, with the family on one side and the footmen and maids on the other, but Corona could not remember it ever being played. The only notes of comfort she could recall were the beautiful carriage rugs made from the skins of cats that strayed up from the village and were shot by the 'keepers. Necton did have a walled park, an Italian garden with statues of cupids and goddesses and an elegant but decaying Palladian orangery, which were all good places to explore. The children occupied a nursery that seemed a long way from the drawing room to which they were occasionally summoned. Corona found her grandmother forbidding, and her grandfather monosyllabic, unlike her paternal grandfather who would take her on his knee and feed her cream and sugar with a spoon. Sadly, neither house still stands.

Once they were married, Philip and Lilian lived eight miles away at Narborough, in two cottages converted into a house. It is remarkable that although the children often stayed at Necton, Lilian never went back nor did her mother ever come to Narborough Cottage. It was a modest but pretty house, surrounded by pink chestnut trees, adjoining the buildings owned by the malting company of which Philip was Chairman and which provided employment for half the village. Barley was brought in to the Maltings by horse drawn wagons, in 200 lb sacks that had to be unloaded, poured into water troughs to germinate and then spread out to dry on slate floors heated by a furnace.

Being Chairman was not a particularly demanding job, nor a lucrative one. The family lived mostly on Lilian's allowance from her father. Philip was able to spend the summer otter-hunting and the winter shooting. He also took increasingly to heavy drinking but nobody ever mentioned that. Lilian was a splendid horsewoman and hunted all winter, going to meets at neighbouring houses, including the Royal family's house at Sandringham. Corona's sister Rose remembered visits from King

Edward VII and Queen Alexandra to Runcton, their carriage drawn by immaculately groomed white Lippizaners with their manes and tails kept long. She claimed her uncles used to bribe the coachmen to let them drive it through the village while the King and Queen were safely out of sight in the house.

Corona was born on 7th July 1911. She always felt something of an afterthought since her brothers, Billy and Somerville, were ten and eight years older respectively and away at school for much of the time. She did become friends with her sister Rose, but even she was six years older. As soon as she was able to dress herself, Corona would cut a chunk of bread and butter and go out to join the men at work in the Maltings, sometimes being allowed to ride one of the shaft horses for a little way. The water for steeping the barley came from a channel cut across a bend in the River Nar that ran through the village. Rose and Corona spent hours watching trout, motionless among the emerald water weeds apart from the movement of the fins that kept their noses pointing upstream. They caught them with worms and could also catch eels, by manoeuvring a rod through the furnace room windows, and dace, roach and pike, by casting a net into the pool below the cut.

The Maltings was a children's paradise with five floors connected by ladders, and little wicker contraptions on wheels for moving the grain that made wonderful racing chariots. Other outdoor activities included bicycle rides and cricket. Indoors there were card games like Pelmanism and Old Maid, and singing round Lilian's grand piano, with the words of 'My Little Grey Home in the West' always rendered 'The Little Grey Hole in my Vest' by Billy. Their mother read Bible stories to them every day as they lay on the floor. The ones they remembered were Old Testament stories of Daniel in the lions' den, and Jael, who hammered the tent peg into Sisera's temple. They went to church every Sunday, always sitting three pews back from the pulpit, until Corona was seventeen, when she declared with some trepidation that she was not coming. To her surprise, nothing was said.

In fact, Philip seems to have been an indulgent father. When she was nine Corona asked her father to teach her to fish properly, with a fly. Affecting surprise that she could not already do so, he took her off then and there for her first lesson in casting. A few years later, she

suggested to him that if she had a gun she could help keep the rats down in the Maltings. Sure enough, she was given a beautiful little double barrelled .410 for her fourteenth birthday. In that first season of 1925, her meticulously kept game book records six rats, two rabbits, fourteen moorhens and two duck. The following year she shot her first snipe and her first pheasant. Happy days spent fishing, shooting, fox-hunting and otter-hunting followed, all recorded carefully and often illustrated by witty pencil sketches.

The First World War affected Corona more directly than it did Nigel, although his father was away at the Front. Philip became Quartermaster of a stores depot in Reading on the strength of his business experience, and the family rented a house there for a time to be with him. A house in the village was requisitioned as a convalescent home for wounded soldiers and the bored inmates in their blue uniforms used to cheer the chubby little girl (an adjective that may surprise those who only remember the mature Corona's lean and elegant figure) as she was led past on her pony. She watched the ramshackle planes that were based on the flat lands of East Anglia, just a short flight from France. She and Rose both recalled the sadness that pervaded the household when news came that one of the young pilots from Marham Airfield who used to come to tea would not be coming again. They both also remembered seeing a German Zeppelin sailing over the house, presumably searching for Marham.

A local girl called Amy was engaged to teach Corona to read and write. They went on long walks collecting, identifying and colouring

drawings of wild flowers. When she was nine she went to school. She did not flourish and, when one of the teachers moved to Langford Grove in Essex, to start her own school, Corona went with her. She was much happier there, despite the dreadful brown uniform. Corona was no good at English or History but shone at Geography, because she could draw, and Botany, thanks to those walks with Amy. She was good at games, playing lacrosse for the school. However, she left with nothing to show for it all since an attack of acute appendicitis coincided with her School Certificate exams.

She was sent to a finishing school in France, in the countryside near Rouen, to learn to speak French, cook and sew. When she returned home after a year, she volunteered to work as a nursing assistant in the Middlesex Hospital, but it does not seem to have interfered with a busy social life. She used to go to Scotland with her school friend Jane Hickley on shooting, stalking and fishing holidays and also for a rather grander stay up there when her sister Rose was working for the Cliftons of Kidalton on the island of Islay. They dined on Saturday nights off silver plate to the accompaniment of their personal piper.

By 1928, aged seventeen, she was shooting regularly with the Narborough Hall syndicate and also with a neighbouring syndicate run by a London businessman, Jack Hotblack, using her father's 12 bore, and always as a guest, not paying a penny for what she only later recognised to be a great privilege. She bought a horse with a 500 guinea legacy from a cousin, hunted him for three seasons with the West Norfolk Hunt and raced him once in a point-to-point, falling ingloriously about a quarter of the way round. Jack Hotblack invited her on a salmon fishing trip to Norway, during which she was thrilled to catch a fish weighing just under 30 lbs, but not enough to accept his proposal of marriage. She did briefly become engaged to a hunting farmer called Wilfred (Jim) Thomson, but quickly changed her mind.

In 1930, when she was nineteen, her brother Somerville returned from Kenya where he was learning to farm. They did a lot of fishing together and he taught her to tie flies. Tragically, he died on 19th December 1931, shortly after his return to Kenya, aged twenty seven. Worse was to follow when Billy, studying to become an estate agent, crashed his motorcycle on 22nd August 1932. He too was killed. Corona never mentioned the accident afterwards but Joe Lubbock still recalls the devastating effect it had on both girls.

Perhaps it is not surprising that so many of Corona's twenty-first birthday presents reflected her sporting interests, including a hunting whip with her initials in silver and a landing net, intended for the capture of monster trout. Not long afterwards, she and her father went to pay a duty call on the great nephew of a distant cousin who had started up a silver fox farm nearby. Nigel was rather startled to see them, having slept late after being out wildfowling under a full moon most of the previous night, but it was the start of an enduring friendship.

CHAPTER 3:

GREY GEESE AND SILVER FOXES

Wildfowlers pursue their quarry alone, or with one or two like minded companions, along empty and sometimes hostile stretches of marsh and foreshore. It is a winter sport, for ducks and geese are mostly migratory, and the worse the weather the better the 'fowler is pleased. It is often only in conditions of wind, rain, snow or fog, or better still all of them at once, that there is a realistic chance of getting near these truly wild birds. The best bet is when they move from their roosts to where they are feeding at dusk and back again at dawn, or when they take advantage of a full moon to fit in an extra foraging expedition. The 'fowler's tactics then include hiding in creeks or under the sea wall or digging shallow pits in wet mud to conceal his prone body in the hope of intercepting their flight lines. To be successful he must know, or guess correctly, when and where they will fly and be familiar with the tide tables, since on flat ground the incoming tide moves easily fast enough to cut off the unwary from dry land. Success depends on understanding the quarry, knowing the ground and the tides, physical endurance, individual skill and pure luck.

It may come as a surprise to his family and friends to learn that Nigel is still remembered as an icon for English coastal wildfowlers. For the ten years before the war, he spent most of his moons, dawns and dusks on the coast. His annual total of geese was only between fifteen and twenty, not least because he would not shoot them inland on their feeding grounds, but he calculated that he averaged between sixty and a hundred flights a year. He wrote a book, 'Fowler's Moon', published in 1955 and illustrated with Corona's elegant and restrained line drawings, that still resonates strongly with those who pursue this most demanding of sports. Remarkably, it was mostly written with an illegal pencil in very small writing on a roll of loo paper during the three months Nigel spent in solitary confinement in a Gestapo prison in 1944. Philip Gray, a wildfowling author himself, was sufficiently inspired by it to go out to Africa to meet Nigel in 1981. Columnist John Humphreys told his readers in The Shooting Times in August 2007 that the five shillings he spent on a second hand copy of 'Fowler's Moon' was *"the best five bob I ever spent"*. Phil Gray's son, Robert, published Nigel's account of a punt-gunning expedition with Peter Scott in the 100th edition of The Shooting Gazette in February 2000 and named Corona as one of his dream team of guns, along with Ernest Hemingway, in the 200th edition of the magazine in June 2008.

The book describes how a novice wildfowler, Rory, the narrator, learns wildfowling lore and practice from a more experienced friend, a silver fox farmer called William. It is entirely typical of Nigel that he narrates the story from the point of view of the novice, when in real life he was the more experienced William. Rory is probably based on his Cambridge friend Roderick (Rods) Parkyn, who later married Nigel's sister Puss and to whom the book is dedicated. John Humphreys described Nigel's style as modest but thrilling. There are few rhetorical flourishes but you cannot doubt that every incident actually happened to Nigel on the ground and in the conditions that he describes with telling detail. He had experienced the wet and the cold, felt the frustrations redeemed by occasional triumphs and thrilled to the beauty of the fens and the shoreline, and the birds that scrape a living from them. There cannot be many first time authors who could have resisted the temptation to finish the tale of a wildfowler's journey with a triumphant right and left at geese. Nigel's fictional alter ego fumbles his final stalk, misses with both barrels and suffers a furious self-recrimination that strikes a chord immediately with those who have been there.

Nigel discovered wildfowling in 1928, while at Cambridge, spending too much of his winters on the coast for his tutors' entire approval. Corona began in 1931, persuading the brother of a friend of hers to take her duck flighting on the

Norfolk coast. By the time she was twenty two she was competent enough to go by herself, which is how she met Peter Scott. He was the son of Captain Scott of the Antarctic, already an accomplished wildlife artist, who sailed in the 1936 Olympics and later became a dashing Motor Torpedo Boat commander, a champion glider pilot and the founder of The Wildfowl Trust, to be knighted for services to conservation. He was also a contemporary of Nigel's at Cambridge, although that would have meant nothing to Corona when they met. They went wildfowling together once or twice and then, in January 1934, he offered to take her out in his gun punt.

A gun punt does not resemble the flat bottomed punts that Peter and Nigel would have been familiar with as they were poled down the River Cam by nattily dressed undergraduates. Gun punts had to cope with the winds and tides of the North Sea, so they had high gunwales but were still low enough to be invisible in the ideal conditions of a light chop. A single barrelled, large bore shotgun was fixed to the punt, so that the whole craft had to be lined up to take aim. Today the idea of a single shot from a large bore gun accounting for literally dozens of birds seems unsporting. But the knowledge, patience, skill and physical endurance necessary to find the birds, to creep close to them across open water without alarming them, and to manoeuvre the punt into a firing position would be well beyond the capabilities of most of those who today shoot pheasants driven over them by others. The first day Peter took Corona out they were on the water for eleven hours without coming close to a single bird.

They went out again in December 1934 and this time they did locate a raft of widgeon. To get close to the birds it is necessary to lie at full length in the bottom of the punt. The gunner lies behind the huge gun, using a small rod to raise or lower it. The paddler lies behind, on top of the gunner's legs and has to propel the punt towards the quarry and line it up by imperceptible wrist movements with little paddles no bigger than a table tennis bat. Peter allocated Corona the post of gunner, and even at this exciting moment, she was girl enough to feel *"a little shy of my posterior view when lying in the stalking position"* as she confided to her game book afterwards. That was all forgotten when Peter whispered *"Now!"* and she pulled the lanyard. The recoil of the massive gun smashed her knuckle into her too-close face, costing her a lot of blood and half a tooth. To Peter's bewilderment she did not

28

cry, but helped him to collect fifteen widgeon before taking herself off to Lynn Hospital, still covered in mud and wearing thigh boots, to be patched up by a very disapproving female doctor.

Nigel got his chance to go out with Peter a few years later, in February 1937. It was blowing hard and Peter was not hopeful. Nigel assured him that he did not mind rowing and they set out at half past eight in the morning. They covered three or four miles in the driving rain before spotting a raft of several hundred widgeon. They came in to within two hundred yards and then began the final, patient stalk against the wind and rain. Eventually, Peter judged that they were in range. Nigel hesitated a fraction too long before firing but, even so, the bag was forty one birds. They followed a second lot of about a hundred and fifty and, despite some ticklish moments in a brief spell of sunlight that made them feel very conspicuous, collected another twenty. It was now getting choppy, growing dark and they were four or five miles out. Even Nigel was simply too bone tired to get excited about another chance that showed itself just before reaching dry land and safety.

Shortly after Corona and her father called on him, Nigel came across her fishing on the Nar and was impressed by how well she was casting - for a girl. They discovered that they had much in common. They went fishing together on 12th June and shooting on 20th August 1934. They both recorded the day's bag in their respective game books as two duck, one curlew, two pigeons, a little owl and a rabbit. By September there were regular wildfowling forays on the coast as well as evenings spent potting bunnies with a .22 rifle to feed the silver foxes.

On one expedition depicted in Corona's sketch on page 30, they were caught poaching. Corona kept the keeper talking while Nigel searched carefully through his game pocket to ensure that he handed back two old birds rather than two young and tender ones. When his brothers Grey and Guy came up to shoot with him that September, Nigel told them, as nonchalantly as he could in the face of their combined disbelief and derision, that he had invited a girl as well. In the event, Corona quickly won them over by bringing down a flying rook with a .22 rifle, a feat for which the weapon is not

Sep[.] 20th 1934.   FAIRLY CAUGHT !

designed and which demands equal measures of marksmanship, nerve and sheer luck.

Much of what they shot or gathered in other ways would have been destined to feed the silver foxes. Once Nigel and Corona collected ninety nine moorhen's eggs in a day, hopefully taking due note of Nigel's father's rules about the last safe date on which a nest could legitimately be raided. They also had more conventional meetings. Corona persuaded Nigel to accompany her to a dance at the Dawnay's, although they took themselves off for a game of squash halfway through, which necessitated Corona's girding her long dress up into its belt. They also disgraced themselves by completing a flight before changing for the Hunt Ball in January 1936, at which they arrived just after midnight - and with an entirely unappreciated dead goose.

Corona was not entirely dependent on Nigel for her entertainment. In 1935 she went to Finland to spend the summer with a wealthy Finnish family on the condition that she spoke English to them. She found them great fun and partied and travelled with them all round Finland. They quickly learned what she enjoyed and she joined them partridge shooting, was deputed to shoot a crow when they needed meat to bait crayfish lines with and, during a hunt which she remembered for the rest of her life, shot her first and only elk. On the strength of that trip she was invited to stay with a family in Ireland who wanted to hear about fishing in Finland. She took her hunting boots and bowler hat with her and was generously mounted and introduced to Irish hunting. A print of Snaffles' evocative picture of an Irish hunting scene entitled 'Great banks there was' later accompanied her to Africa and hung in the hall at Merryhill.

The following year she went to Berlin to look after two small children but her employers, alarmed by the new Chancellor, Hitler, left for South America. Corona toyed with the idea of staying on, having been offered another job, but did not take to her prospective employer - perhaps unsurprisingly. Herr Himmler, as creator of the SS, later became one of the most feared men in Nazi Germany. Instead she spent the summer of 1936 sailing off the coast of Stockholm with friends.

Corona always said that she fell for Nigel the moment she saw him, but she had no indication of what he felt until he proposed to her. She was startled enough to need twenty four hours to think about it but, on 31st May 1937, Nigel was able to send the telegram that is still preserved in his mother's scrap book: *"PLEASE BOTH YOU AND MUM WAIT UP TONIGHT AND PLEASE HAVE SPARE ROOM AND MINE READY . NIGEL"*.

They were married on 20th September 1937 at Narborough. Nigel's brothers came up for the wedding of course, and his youngest brother Guy used to recount how they all went out to try and get Nigel to shoot a partridge before getting him to church, all dressed up in what Nigel's game book calls their "wedding kit". Inevitably the birds proved elusive but eventually one gave Nigel a chance. He hit it but did not kill it and it disappeared over the hedge. They had run out of time but the keeper and his dog - and that can only have been Harry, who helped Nigel look after the silver foxes, and Nigel's spaniel Bill - set off after it. Sure enough when Nigel and Corona emerged from Narborough Church, married, there at the back of the little crowd on the pavement was Harry, triumphantly waving a dead partridge. Whether it was actually Nigel's bird nobody ever knew.

Corona had no such happy distractions. Escorted into church by no less than six adult bridesmaids, she hated every minute of it. Nigel wore the wrong sort of stock, the address by the cousin who married them was puerile and, to cap it all, because money was tight, there was no champagne but only tea and coffee. That first night was spent in a borrowed cottage on the coast, enlivened by their carelessly putting a live rocket, which they had collected with the driftwood, onto the fire. For their honeymoon they went shooting in Scotland, accompanied by Nigel's spaniel, Bill. Bill appears in 'Fowler's Moon' under his own name but is rather unkindly described as *"a liver and tan spaniel - at least, the new arrival was more like a spaniel than any other breed that I could think of. Nevertheless, an attractive hound; there was plenty of breadth between those friendly eyes, and later I had good cause to marvel at his working powers."*

They returned to live in Nigel's pre-fabricated house, which they referred to as the Rabbit Hutch, financially supported by an allowance from Nigel's parents. There they were soon joined by Robin, born at Wyecliffe on 5th October 1938, who nearly had an early baptism of fire when Corona only just stopped a furious Nigel from discharging a gun over the sleeping baby at a skein of providentially fog-bound geese flying low over the house. Behind the house stood the pens for his foxes. Silver foxes are a domestic variant of the North American red fox, handsome and graceful beasts, with orange tawny eyes set in black masks, bred for their astonishingly soft and beautiful silver grey fur. Nigel looked after them with the help of Harry Mullenger, a local man who badly needed a job, having lost his left hand in a shooting accident but receiving nothing from his insurers on the grounds that he should not have been shooting on a Sunday. Harry too appears under his own name in 'Fowler's Moon'. *"Ostensibly, Harry helped look after the foxes and did odd jobs. In fact he did, and more, for he looked upon the foxes as his own and took a fitting pride in them. In addition to that and the thousand and one odd jobs that kept on cropping up, he spent most of his spare time in keepering William's little shoot. Fixed working hours he had none, but he did about twice as much as any man I've ever met when work was needed. William and he were far more partners than master and man, and Harry's loyalty was absolute."* So much so that, during the war, whenever Corona wanted him to do something, she had to pretend she had heard from Nigel, asking for it to be done.

And war was coming. Nigel had no desire to be a Regular soldier as two of his brothers, Mytton and Guy, already were but he knew that if war came he, like other Thornycrofts before him, would have to do his bit. He joined his local Territorial Army unit, 5th Battalion The Royal Norfolk Regiment, and trained with them two nights a week. Even after that exhausting day with Peter Scott he had to dash off and change into uniform *"to try and look wise and teach wretched soldiers things they knew a damn sight more about than I did. How I kept awake I don't know. I certainly couldn't concentrate with pictures of widgeon and grebes and divers and all manner of ducks, flying, swimming and running in front of my eyes."*

CHAPTER 4:

NIGEL'S WAR

In August 1939 the Territorial Army was mobilised. Nigel was posted to a new 7th Battalion of The Royal Norfolk Regiment to be employed as Pioneers. Pioneers assist the fighting Battalions by digging trenches and anti-tank ditches, laying mines and wire and so on. Later in the war a Royal Pioneer Corps was formed but at the outset each Division was allocated a Territorial Army Battalion to perform the role. 7th Norfolks was attached, by a War Office official with a sense of humour, to the 51st Highland Division. The men of The Black Watch, Seaforth, Gordon, Cameron and Argyll and Sutherland Highlanders could hardly have come from a more different background to their Pioneers, raised on the flat farmlands of Norfolk.

By the beginning of 1940, 51st Highland Division was trained but still equipped with indifferent weaponry and very green. In April they were sent for a tour of duty along the River Saar, under French command, to give them operational experience. The Pioneers were kept busy. To put their position into a state of defence, 4th Camerons alone needed 80,000 sandbags, 2000 A frames, 2000 sheets of revetting material, 600 coils of barbed wire and 1200 wiring pickets, which all had to be brought up on mules before it could be used.

The 'Phoney War' came to an abrupt end in May 1940 when first Holland and then Belgium surrendered to the Germans, freeing seven Panzer Divisions for the invasion of France. 51st Highland Division, still under French command, was thrown into their path. It was a time of order, counter-order and sometimes disorder. As losses whittled down their strength, the Brigades and Battalions of 51st Highland Division could no longer cover the frontages they were being asked to. 7th Norfolks stopped being a Pioneer Battalion and was incorporated into an extra, composite fighting Brigade but the front was still too wide and the defenders too few to stem the tide of German tanks. The Division relinquished no ground without fighting but nevertheless slowly fell back. Each time they got to a new position, tired soldiers started to dig in, only to get new orders to move again, not only wasting their dwindling resources of energy but using up precious opportunities for rest. The delay they imposed allowed the rest of the British Expeditionary Force, and thirty thousand French soldiers, to be evacuated from Dunkirk, but on 8th June two Panzer Divisions appeared behind the Highlanders. That was their last chance to break for Le Havre where the Royal Navy was waiting to evacuate them. They could have done so, but only at the cost of abandoning the French, who did not have the same availability of motor transport. That would have destroyed the alliance and the Division was ordered to hold on.

By 11th June, when they were finally ordered to head for the coast, it was too late. 7th Norfolks dug in to hold the port of St Valery while the evacuation started but, before more than a thousand men had been taken off, the French commander surrendered. A Seaforth officer wrote later: *"the clear notes of a bugle sounded in St Valery's smouldering pit - "Cease Fire". It couldn't be! Only two hours before I had heard the General threaten to shoot a Frenchman if he didn't take his white flag down from the Church. Then I saw the Brigade Major. "Does this apply to us, Sir?"... "I'm afraid it does". Tears, floods of tears, rage and bloody fury. The enemy appeared... They separated us from the men. We were herded into a field and left to lie there. Unbelievably tired but with no wish to sleep. More officers arrived. We were just rubbish, no use to anyone but our own futile selves."*

They were marched off, still separated from their men, into captivity. The first day they covered twenty five miles. There was little food or water for them or indeed for their German guards, and no permanent accommodation, or plans for any, since Hitler believed that he would be in London by Christmas. They marched two hundred and twenty miles in the next fourteen days, apart from two short stages by lorry, marching sixteen to twenty miles a day, in a column of about three hundred British and French soldiers. They spent the nights in open fields, in barns, churches, schools, factories (where they slept on the storage racks), or barracks. The only meal of the day came at the end of the march, occasionally supplemented by what could be obtained from the French, Belgian and Dutch civilians through whose countries they passed, or by digging up root vegetables or dandelions. They had a rest day at Aalst, where they were able to wash their clothes and where Nigel wrote Corona a letter which she eventually received ten months later on 28th April 1941. In Holland they were allowed to bathe in the sea before being loaded onto steamers for a hundred and thirty mile trip up the Rhine, carrying a loaf of bread each for the two day journey. The last five hundred miles were by train across Germany, a crowded two and a half days with little chance of food or sleep.

By 7th July, bearing the number 1406, Nigel found himself in an officer only camp, Oflag VIIC at Laufen, from which he eventually moved via a short stay in Oflag VIB to Oflag VIIB, at Eichstätt in southern Germany which he reached in August 1942. Life in the camps was characterised by permanent hunger, stultifying boredom, and black feelings of helplessness and uselessness. Non-co-operation by prisoners of war with their German guards has been trivialised by post war books and films as an amusing game, but it was a psychological necessity to prevent young and, until recently, active men, used to making rapid and vital decisions on behalf of those under their command, from slipping into depression and self-loathing. It had to be carefully judged. Even at Eichstätt, a comparatively humanely run camp, the Commandant, goaded beyond endurance, confiscated all the furniture and mattresses for a period of two months in 1944, making a wearisome existence almost unbearable. But 'Goon-baiting', as Nigel and his peers described it, gave the prisoners the essential little victories that sustained their self-belief, and also provided a distraction from the activities of those planning to escape, the so-called 'tally-ho boys', of whom Nigel was one.

By the time he had been in prison for four years, he calculated he had taken part in eleven escape attempts of one sort or another, some opportunistic and others the outcome of months of meticulous planning and preparation by committees dedicated to the provision of clothes, maps, compasses, food and some means of carrying it. The eleventh scheme featured a tunnel. It took six months to dig and required the clandestine disposal of seventy tons of earth. Forty two prisoners were organised into four gangs, one to provide security by 'stooging', one to dig, one to dispose of the spoil and one to rest. The diggers could only work for half an hour at a time in the confines of a hole nineteen inches by twenty four, scraping rather than digging because of the need for silence.

Despite no less than six changes of direction caused by disheartening encounters with solid rock, they were eventually able to push a discreet stick through a patch of soil visible from inside the wire and just where they expected it to be.

At that triumphant moment they heard of the break out of seventy six officers, mostly RAF, from Stalag Luft III at Sagan - later filmed as 'The Great Escape' - that ended with the recapture and murder of fifty of them by machine gun fire. The escape was called off and the tunnel lay unused for an anxious and ill-tempered month. Eventually a reduced escape attempt by just eight men was agreed and Nigel was one of the eight selected. They chose a date that meant there would be little or no moon for the following week and broke through into the rain and the darkness at eleven o'clock at night. The plan was to go out at five minute intervals, meet up at a rendezvous a mile or so away and then walk to the Swiss border, travelling in pairs, by night and across country for two hundred and fifty kilometres. Nigel was the third man out. As he headed for the woods he heard shots, saw the searchlights come on, and then heard more shots. He waited for his partner at the rendezvous for three hours and then set out alone.

It was still raining. For almost two weeks he had to avoid roads, bridges and buildings and never succeeded in drying himself, his clothes or his kit properly. He walked about thirteen kilometres a night and lay up in woods by day. He occasionally found something extra to eat, such as seed potatoes or snails, once taking five eggs from a yellowhammer's nest, and twice killing a small bird with a catapult, but the night is not a good time for hunting and he could not move by day. It was seldom safe to light a fire because wet wood makes smoke and there was no dry wood. And still it went on raining.

He kept sane during the days, when he had to lie still without making any noise or smoke, often with people working in the woods quite close to him, by writing a journal describing the trees, flowers, birds and insects that he could see, or often only hear, from his circumscribed little patch of the world. It was intended for, and occasionally directly addressed to, Corona. It is telling, despite the hardihood and frequent exposure to cold and wet that characterised his wildfowling years, how often he refers to his discomfort. Four years of inadequate diet and no exercise were not a good preparation for so demanding an expedition. On the third day he confided to his journal that he had pretty nearly had it. He hit a new low on the fifth day with the discovery that over half his little store of biscuit had got wet and gone mouldy and when on the seventh day he found that his watch, a wedding present from Corona, had stopped, it hit him hard. Finally, that night the rain stopped and hard walking meant he was almost dry by the morning of the eighth day.

He felt restored enough to spend an hour and a half working mutton fat into his boots and to shave properly, not with the muddy water wrung out of his trousers that he had had to use before. For the first time he allowed himself to speculate in his journal on his chances of making it to the Swiss border next week or the week after, and he expressed his amazement at the advice he had often been given to take a book or be driven mad by boredom. He claimed he could happily have spent twice as long watching and listening to the birds.

The ninth and tenth days he made good progress and sounded as though he was beginning to enjoy his adventure but on the night of the tenth day the weather turned nasty again. The following morning he repeated the ominous phrase that he had almost had it. He was exhausted, hungry, ill and constantly wet, and he was not certain that he had the physical strength to make it to the border. The country was pretty demanding by now with steep and winding valleys in which he got lost twice on the twelfth night, cutting the effective distance achieved by half.

His thirteenth night on the run he described as crowded. As he set out, he spotted and successfully avoided a forester but failed to deceive his dog. The forester was armed and Nigel was unable to argue. He was marched to the village of Grotyngen, where they woke a rather cross Burgermeister (Mayor). Nigel's pack was taken off him, and he was searched and locked up in a little room about six feet by eight. The search had not been very thorough and he had managed to conceal his knife behind the talc that covered his map. Once alone, he set about cutting out the lock. He laboured for an hour with little result except two burst and bleeding blisters and turned in despair to the window.

By sheer strength he shifted one bar enough to reveal that the mortar holding it was old. Using the faintly ridiculous gadget for picking stones out of a horse's hoof that all knives used to have, he succeeded in unpicking enough mortar to remove the whole window frame and quickly eased through it. He calculated he had at least eight days to go to the Swiss border and to have any chance at all he had to have his pack. So he went round to the front door, and, using his horse's hoof picker again, proceeded to break back in! Luck was with him for he found the pack un-tampered with and as he resumed his road the church clock told him it was still only one o'clock in the morning, just two and a half hours since the dog had winded him.

Such luck could not last. Just before the next village he ran into the arms of two soldiers looking for escaped Russian prisoners from a nearby camp. They hauled him off to wake another Burgermeister, this one a twinkling little man with a pretty daughter who sent for bread and cider and who sat up with Nigel until half past four in the morning, swapping fishing stories. As dawn broke he opened the shutters to show Nigel in the distance, blue and dim but real and visible, the Swiss mountains for which he had been making.

A policeman escorted Nigel to the nearest town. They got on famously, the policeman sharing his bread and a huge radish and trying to teach Nigel the names of trees in German. Nigel felt a bit guilty as he stretched out his long legs until the old man was fairly dripping with sweat, hoping to dodge him in the woods. He might have saved himself the trouble for the woods turned out to be full of Hitler Youth on a training exercise. At Ehingen the local police roared with laughter at his tale of the discomfiture of the first Burgermeister. From there he was taken by train to Ulm, ruefully watching landmarks flash by that he had so recently traversed laboriously in the dark. At Ulm he was stripped, searched, rather more professionally this time, questioned for three hours and finally handed over to the Gestapo.

There followed three months of slow starvation in solitary confinement. Nigel says little about them in his journal except to note that he went in weighing twelve stone and came out weighing nine and incapable of walking more than fifty yards. He got ten minutes exercise three times a week when he could see, but not talk to, other prisoners. The only time they could exchange a few words was when Allied air raids forced them into the cellars. They were mostly Russians but there were some from almost every country of Europe, including Germans imprisoned for crimes such as listening to British radio broadcasts. Nigel was interviewed twice by interrogation teams from Berlin, frightening performances that for some reason stopped short of physical violence, although he occasionally heard the cries of others.

After twelve weeks the prison doctor told Nigel he was likely to die if he could not get him returned to military, rather than Gestapo, custody. On the eighty seventh day the miracle happened and Nigel was sent back to Eichstätt. He could not walk the mile from the station to the camp and the German Army Commandant expressed his shame at the way he had been treated by the Gestapo, who were hated and feared by the German Army as much as by anybody. He had been away for exactly one hundred days.

News of the invasion of Europe in June 1944 did wonders for prisoners' morale but it also presented a very real problem. The British War Office took the view that the German guards would treat their prisoners well in the knowledge that they would shortly be the winning side. That optimism took a knock when the German Army handed over responsibility for the camps to Himmler, the Gestapo and the SS, presumably to be used as hostages or bargaining counters in subsequent peace negotiations. War Office instructions that prisoners should stay put and do nothing to annoy their guards looked rather foolish when the camps began to be emptied and their inmates marched out to unknown destinations. Nigel and several others decided to stay put when Oflag VIIB was emptied.

They amassed enough food and water to keep them alive for a month and simply hid in one of the attics when the rest of the prisoners were formed up on 14th April 1945 and marched out. Tragically, the column of marching prisoners was attacked by Allied aircraft, presumably under the impression that they were retreating German soldiers. Half a dozen American P-47 Thunderbolts, each with eight wing mounted machine guns, made no less than five passes over them, killing eight, wounding forty one and enabling about a dozen to make a break. The remaining prisoners were brought back into camp for twenty four hours to recover and some of Nigel's group decided to go with them when they left again the following day. This time, he was one of only three hiding in his attic when he restarted his journal.

Once again he watched and wrote about the birds he could see through a hole in the tiles but also had the movement of troops and tanks, and the noise of aircraft, gunfire and larger explosions to record and puzzle over. When the empty camp was filled with Russian prisoners, Nigel's group managed to contact and befriend three of them, which enabled them to leave their attic for a little comparatively fresh air some nights. After eleven days and nights in hiding, and having seen and heard American tanks on the edge of the town, they smartened themselves up as best they could, marched up to the demoralised German guards and demanded to be let out. They were!

They lay up in the town of Eichstätt while it was being fought over. Towards the end of the day, a Jeep driven by an American, but containing a British RAF officer, appeared. They told him what they knew of the situation in the town and the American, who, miraculously, turned out to be a four star General, identified by Nigel as General Mark Clark in his journal, drove them seventy miles to Nuremberg and flew them in his private aircraft to Rheims where he was due for a conference with General Eisenhower. Nigel was back in England eighteen hours after hailing the Jeep. It took a frustrating further two days of red tape before he was allowed the last few miles home, but, after all, there was a war on.

CHAPTER 5:
CORONA'S WAR

Corona's war started pretty badly. After seeing Nigel off, she returned to Narborough to have her second baby, a daughter whose name we do not know. Her sister, Rose, was with her and a great comfort in the three terrible days before the baby died. Soon afterwards their father broke his hip and was taken into Norwich Hospital, from which he never came out. Their mother had to leave the house at Narborough as it belonged to the company and the new Chairman needed it. She went to live in a hotel in Edinburgh to be near Rose, who was in a teaching order of nuns there.

Then Corona learnt that the 51st Highland Division had surrendered at St Valery. Peter Scott, now Robin's Godfather, had been part of the Naval escort waiting unavailingly to take the Division off and had landed briefly, but did not run into Nigel, who was apparently off trying to blow up a German tank on the outskirts of the town. Three months of anxious waiting followed before she was notified by the War Office that he was alive and a prisoner and received his first letter. As the system settled down, the Red Cross undertook to get one parcel a month to each prisoner, containing clothes, food and razor blades when they could be obtained. Not all of the parcels got through but they were a psychological as well as a physical lifeline for the prisoners, as deprived of family contact as they were of food. Some letters reached Nigel as well, including one which his Deakin grandmother, to save

her arthritic fingers, had typed so ineptly that Nigel was summoned to the Camp Commandant's office to explain the apparently coded communication with its randomly scattered asterisks and exclamation marks.

For most of the war, Corona and Robin stayed at Wyecliffe with Nigel's mother and father, having let the Rabbit Hutch to an RAF Lieutenant and left Harry in charge of the silver foxes. Once a year she would go back to see that all was well and to oversee the killing and skinning of the year's crop. She and Robin occasionally went to spend a few days in Cheshire with Nigel's friend and wildfowling partner, Rods Parkyn, and his parents. They lived close enough to Manchester for Corona to feel the ground shake on the occasion that it was bombed whilst they were staying there. Rods had not been allowed to join the Services since his work as an engineer was deemed to be valuable to the war effort, so he volunteered as a firewatcher and worked nights as well as days.

Two of Nigel's brothers, Mytton and Guy, were already in the Army. Grey now joined The Royal Engineers and Patricia The Women's Royal Naval Service, universally known as the Wrens. Corona and her mother-in-law, whom she adored, felt compelled to do their bit too. Vida contributed generously to appeals for scrap metal to aid the war effort, only just being dissuaded by a friend from including some rather fine family silver. Corona worked every morning in what had been a coach building factory in Hereford, filing rough edges off aluminium parts for Lancaster bombers. It was a four mile bicycle ride each way. Vida looked after Robin on those mornings until he started nursery school, after which Corona would drop him off on her way to the factory. At first, she was one of only two women working there and when they found they could easily do more than the laid down minimum in order to get a bit of overtime pay, they were warned by the men that they should not make the job look too easy or the minimum requirement for everybody would go up. Corona was soon moved onto working a lathe, then a drill and, after a couple of years, into the inspection team.

It was at the factory that she received an entirely unexpected bouquet of red roses labelled *"from Nigel"* on their wedding anniversary in 1943. It turned out that one of his fellow prisoners had a sister, whom he had tasked to send them in one of his letters home. Letters arrived from time to time from Nigel but not, of course, while he was on the run. During one of these silences, Corona managed to meet a very sick prisoner from Nigel's camp who had been sent home on exchange. The unfortunate man knew that Nigel had been part of an escape attempt that had gone wrong and he assumed that he had been shot, but felt it was not up to him to tell the widow. It must have been a frustrating interview for Corona and a difficult one for the ex-prisoner. Corona realised that he was not telling her everything he knew and she poured out her feelings for Nigel in a letter that she did not expect him ever to read. Happily, it was waiting for him when he emerged from his three months of solitary confinement.

She found herself feeling almost light-hearted at this stage of the war, which she could not understand, until she learnt that Nigel was praying for her happiness every night from his Gestapo cell. Corona, Patricia and Vida regularly used to bicycle the four miles to Hereford, with their bicycle lamps reduced to the merest slits of light to avoid attracting enemy aircraft, to go to the cinema. Charlie and Vida made Wyecliffe available for officers from the colonies with nowhere else to go for their leave and Corona got plenty of shooting and games of squash with them. By 1943 there were American troops in England preparing for the invasion of Europe and those in the camps around Hereford used to give dances, offering food such as their guests had not seen in years, although the household at Wyecliffe was better off than most because of the steady supply of game from the shoot at Brinsop. Corona was escorted to plays and concerts by American officers, including a performance of 'Hamlet' by a young Richard Burton, who later became one of the greatest British actors of his generation.

Then tragedy caught up with the family again. Grey, trained as an engineer at Loughborough, loved his life in The Royal Engineers and was never happier than when dreaming up explosive devices and booby traps. He was killed in North Africa on 26th April 1943 while following up the retreating Axis forces after the Battle of El Alamein. He is buried near Tunis. Patricia, stationed with the Wrens on the Isle of Wight, was bombed twice and buried in rubble on one occasion but without serious injury. Mytton, who had married briefly and divorced, married again, only to find his wife dead one afternoon at Wyecliffe, from cancer of the throat. He went over to Europe shortly afterwards with The Monmouthshire Regiment and was killed in Belgium on 12th September 1944. He is buried at Limburg. The youngest brother, Guy, was also in Europe, having led a company of The King's Shropshire Light Infantry ashore during the D Day landings that initiated the Allied invasion. A surprisingly compassionate War Office, aware that his parents had already lost two sons and had one in captivity, sent him home to England to attend the Staff College.

As the war drew to its end and the possibility of seeing Nigel again grew, the tension and anxiety in case it did not happen became greater and greater. Corona was in Norfolk in April 1945 when the longed for telephone call came. Nigel was back. They agreed that he would go straight to his parents' home at Wyecliffe and she set out to join him there. He tried to meet her en route at Worcester. She found an earlier train that went via Gloucester. When they finally met, both were exhausted by the frustrations and anticlimaxes of that weary journey across wartime England.

Nigel had been in prison for almost five years. At first, Corona found him remarkably unchanged. She noticed that he was suffering from severe vitamin deficiencies that gave him itchy skin. He tended to talk much faster than he used to and he could not pass by a sticky bun in a confectioner's shop without dashing in to buy and eat it. She found herself absurdly possessive and jealous of his need to be with and talk to his father.

What Nigel wanted most was to get out on the foreshore wildfowling. He and Corona found a little cottage in Anglesey in North Wales and got away for a much needed but somehow unsatisfactory break. When they returned to the Lodge at Wyecliffe, which Charlie had made available for them, it was to find that Nigel had been posted to the Middle East, having had just six weeks leave. He went to see his General who, accepting that Nigel was not a career soldier, generously offered him the post of his aide de camp, based at Abergavenny, in Wales. Nigel and Corona jumped at the chance. They spent a year there, and it quickly became clear that neither of them was going to enjoy the peacetime Army.

On the 6th June 1946, Nigel was appointed a Member of The Order of The British Empire (MBE) for his successful escape.

They discussed moving out to New Zealand to farm, but found that there was a three year queue of returning servicemen with the same idea. The family suggested British Columbia but Nigel and Corona favoured Southern Rhodesia (now Zimbabwe), where Nigel had an aunt. In the end, the family agreed to pay for them to go out to British Columbia to have a look but, if they wanted to go on to Rhodesia, they would have to pay for that themselves. Corona's mother came down from Edinburgh to look after Robin and a new baby, Michael, who was born on 5th October 1946, eight years to the day after his brother Robin. Corona, as the practice was then, had to spend a week in hospital with the new arrival, so Nigel took the opportunity to go off to the Solway estuary for a week's wildfowling. He returned on the last day of her stay, still covered in mud, to lay a triumphant goose on her hospital bed.

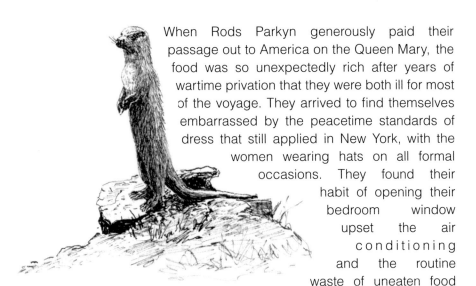

When Rods Parkyn generously paid their passage out to America on the Queen Mary, the food was so unexpectedly rich after years of wartime privation that they were both ill for most of the voyage. They arrived to find themselves embarrassed by the peacetime standards of dress that still applied in New York, with the women wearing hats on all formal occasions. They found their habit of opening their bedroom window upset the air conditioning and the routine waste of uneaten food simply appalled them. When Nigel was taken fishing he disconcerted his hosts by putting back every fish that he did not think was big enough to keep. They were glad to take the long train journey up to British Columbia across what they regarded as flat, monotonous and depressing country.

By the time they got to British Columbia they were short of funds. Nigel got a job laying roofs and Corona became companion and driver to an old lady. They looked at several farms and properties but most of them were small, family sized concerns that offered little more than subsistence farming. It would not do. They set off again, down to Miami and then across to Trinidad where they had a blissfully hot week waiting for a ship to South Africa. With a new continent to discover, no home or job in immediate prospect and two small children already at home, it was disconcerting to learn that Corona was pregnant again. Apart from that discovery, it was an uneventful voyage. One night they found a hawk moth in their cabin while dressing for dinner. Nigel placed it on Corona's shoulder where she wore it as a lovely, living brooch all evening without anyone noticing, or at least commenting.

Once at Cape Town they were looked after by hospitable friends of friends until they were ready to go on up to Rhodesia to meet Nigel's Aunt Gwendolin, his father's sister. Aunt G, as she was known, was married to Commander Wentworth Margesson RN and they had carved a tobacco farm out of the Rhodesian bush when he left the

Navy. Nigel and Corona felt that this was a real possibility for them and the decision was made. They returned to England, to find Mike had grown from a baby into a little boy. He and Corona came back out in October to stay with Aunt G, for the arrival of the new baby, Pip, who was born on the last day of 1947. Nigel and Robin sold up and came out to join them three months later. As he closed the 1947 season in his game book, Nigel was remembering Wyecliffe and the Brinsop shoot. *"Alas, the estate is now up for sale. It is a shoot crammed with happy memories. Robin and I sailed from Venice on Jan 7 to rejoin C and make our home in Southern Rhodesia. Mum, Dad and Puss to follow".*

Nigel, February 1912.

*In Camp, 1915
Charlie with Mytton and Nigel.*

*Puss, Vida, Guy, Charlie, Nigel,
Mytton and 'Shot'.*

*Granny Deakin with
Nigel (on floor), Grey, Guy
and Mytton (seated).*

*Philip and Lilian Gurney circa
1900 at Runcton Hall with Tenby
who used to travel on the trams
by himself to escort Philip home
from work each day.*

*Corona's first salmon, 15lbs, 1932
- caught on the River Usk, Wales.*

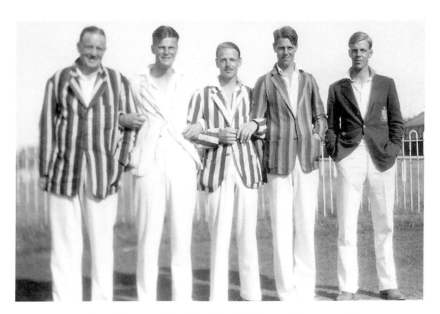

Hereford Gents: Charlie, Nigel, Mytton, Grey and Guy.

Wyecliffe

Wedding Day, Narborough, 20th September 1937.

With Robin.

Nigel wildfowling.

Corona wildfowling.

*Shooting on the Brecon Beacons,
Wales, late 1930s
Corona, Grey, Nigel and Guy.*

In wartime factory
overalls, with Robin.

Shooting lunch at Brinsop, 1942
Mytton, Charlie, Corona and Grey.

Prisoner-of-War
Camp, Oflag
V11B Eichstätt,
1942-45.

Nigel and fellow prisoners-of-war,
Southern Germany, 1942-1945.

Nigel and Robin
on the Solway Estuary.

With Richard and Dillo in tobacco lands, Merryhill, mid 1950s.

Hereford cattle on Merryhill.

Nigel

Curing tobacco in the Merryhill barns.

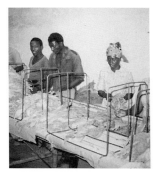

Newspaper clipping of drought tobacco years.

Shona workers grading tobacco.

With Pip and Dillo, early 1950s.

Corona with Pip, Dillo, Mike and Richard (seated).

Crop sprayer on tobacco lands.

Corona with all five sons.

Unloading tobacco barns, Merryhill, 1990.

'Googly' the hippo playing hide & seek with the dogs, Scott's Dam.

Richard, Dillo, Pip, Mike and Robin.

Nigel gutting his trout on the Gairezi.

*Wedza Country Club
cricket team, 1977.*

*Dillo and Corona
walking on Merryhill.*

Mike, Nigel and Pip.... merits of a pump-gun.

At the Gairezi Fisherman's Cottage.

Mike and Richard spearfishing on the Zambezi.

Robin and Corona – expedition up the Kariba Gorge from A Camp.

*Nigel, Pip, Dillo and Gordon Milne
armed and ready for a fishing trip on the Gairezi.*

Nigel on verandah of new house, Scott's Dam.

Dressed up for a family wedding.

Nigel in reflective pose.

*Crossing Scott's on the occasion of Corona and Nigel's
Golden Wedding Anniversary.*

Baobab, A Camp, Zambezi. *Drift over the Pungwe River, Inyanga.*

*En-route to Kariba
or the Zambezi...*

Golden Wedding Anniversary.

50 years of being together...

*Guineafowl shooting
with Bill 1.*

*Game watching on
the Zambezi.*

Nigel, Corona and Mike, new Merryhill homestead.

*Corona and Rosanne,
Zambezi Valley.*

*Corona in new Merryhill House
sittingroom.*

Corona sketching at World's View, Inyanga.

CHAPTER 6
CREATING THE FARM

Nigel's first job was as a learner assistant on a farm at Goromondzi. There was a lot to learn. Nigel had no common language with the workers on the farm and used a horse to get him round which he had no great affinity with either. His one success was accidental. He was asked by his employer to reduce the stealing of fruit from the orchard that surrounded the house. He remarked, in the hearing of an African farm worker who spoke a little English, that it was a pity they could not spray the trees with something to give thieves a stomach ache and the thefts stopped immediately.

There was little future for them at Goromondzi and when they were offered a job managing a farm at Beatrice, they accepted quickly. However, Beatrice proved to be in flat and uninteresting country, with a red soil that impregnated everything, not least the children's clothes. Nor was it easy to make friends with their mostly Afrikaans neighbours. When Charlie, Vida and Patricia sold Wyecliffe and came out to make their home with them, Nigel found he had little time to spare for them.

Charlie became ill and died on 25th October 1948. He is buried in the Anglican Cathedral in Harare. Vida returned to England with those of the family possessions, such as the billiard table, that neither Nigel nor Patricia could give a home to.

It had been an anxious and busy period of which they have left little record but Nigel and Corona's chance to buy a farm of their own finally came. They had heard from a cricketing contact of Nigel's that there was a farm for sale in the Wedza district. It was not a farm at all, really, simply 3,000 acres of untouched bush with a single borehole and a hand pump. It belonged to Walter and Peggy Mundell, who had been farming tobacco and beef cattle since 1930 on four properties, but this one they had never got round to doing much with. Nigel and Corona liked the country and the farm and moved onto it in 1949.

They named it Merryhill, after the Herefordshire wood that had given both of them so much pleasure. Nigel described it in his game book as *"sandy soil & not much game, bar buck. But I fancy we may make something of it & it's a healthy spot, nice neighbours and not too outrageous in price! Anyhow, after three and a half months in Walter's grading shed we moved in on Dec 31. Home at last."* In September 1966 they effectively doubled their acreage by buying a neighbouring farm called Sheffield.

Merryhill and Sheffield were open savannah, dotted with 'msasa' and 'munondo' trees. The frequent granite koppies were home to monkeys and 'dassies' (rock hyrax), and the more open areas held kudu, reedbuck, bush pig, duiker and baboons. With the exception of the baboons, which could ruin seven or eight acres of tobacco in a single visit, and the pigs, which destroyed the maize, Nigel loved to see wildlife on the farm. When a leopard took up residence on one of the koppies and reared her cubs there for several years, taking a steady toll of Nigel's calves, he decided that it was a fair rent for the baboons and monkeys that he hoped she was also taking. Kudu could be a scourge of young tobacco plants but Nigel was happy to let these beautiful antelope have their share. Even the crocodiles that came to live in the dam by the house were welcomed, if nothing else as a deterrent to illegal fishing, until one of them made the mistake of taking one of Corona's Pekingese dogs. Nigel stalked it for several days before killing it with a well-placed shot that made it rear dramatically into the air before dropping to the ground dead, a scene that was faithfully and excitedly re-enacted for weeks afterwards by the farm workers who had witnessed it.

There were guinea fowl and francolin on the farms, and wildfowl came to them as more dams were built. However, Nigel found guinea fowl very ordinary shooting, and knob-billed duck dull and heavy compared to the wildfowl of his former life. He lamented that *"Alas, this isn't a shooting country, but it's fun carrying a gun all the same."* He attempted to introduce pheasants and 'chukor' (the red-legged partridge native to the Himalayas) that he felt would provide more exciting sport, but they proved unable to cope with the sheer weight of predators that they found ranged against them. In 1976 he and three neighbours were more successful in re-introducing impala to the area, acquiring over a hundred beasts from the Game Department and releasing them on their four farms in bunches of twenty to twenty five. They were still thriving when Merryhill was eventually taken by 'war veterans' in 2002.

Nigel's game book peters out before the end of the 1950 season, although he certainly did not stop shooting. During the season, which began on 1st May, there was generally a Saturday shoot on Merryhill or on one of the neighbouring farms belonging to the Travers, the Hamiltons, the Seagers or the Gebbies, often ending with a duck flight. Nigel also looked forward to an annual trip to Shangani in Matabeleland to shoot guinea fowl with Chicken Johnson, and later his son Willie Jim. The fig jam and the banter were all part of the attraction. Nigel's speed and accuracy with a gun was widely admired, although once age started to slow him down, he could sometimes be heard across the water, savagely cursing any failure to meet his own exacting standards.

At times the farms were beautiful with flame lilies, orchids, everlasting flowers and red hot pokers but there were also times of the year when little flourished in the dust and the heat. There was no shortage of insect life, much of it seeming to collect each night in the loo with a light that could not be switched off. However, Corona noticed that as the land was progressively cleared and pesticides made an impact, insect screens and nets became less necessary. Snakes were frequent visitors, particularly to the spare room, which was next to a large clump of bamboos. However, it was regarded as rather poor taste to mention it and most of those that came in from the cold were harmless enough.

They borrowed barns from Walter Mundell for their first season, one to live in and others for their first crop of tobacco. In those days, tobacco was planted as soon as the rains came in November. Nigel and Corona had no seedlings and Corona had to drive round the area begging for neighbours' surplus plants, which were willingly given. Six to ten weeks later, the plants would be topped off to encourage lateral growth, and then reaped, by hand, two or three leaves at a time. These were taken back to the barns and tied onto sticks about four foot long, called 'mateppes', that were passed from hand to hand, up tier after tier of racks, until the tall barn was full of drying leaf hanging in rows from the roof to the floor. The tobacco was cured over a period of about a week in the carefully controlled heat from a wood or coal fired furnace. At the height of the harvest that meant everyone working until nine or ten at night but Corona remembered the barns as happy places with everyone singing as they worked, the voices falling into parts automatically - until the radio took over.

Once they had built their own barns and grading shed on Merryhill, the next priority was a house. Somewhat unusually for a European family, Nigel and Corona chose a local building technique, 'pole and daga'. That involved putting gum poles as close together as possible along both external and internal walls and then working puddled earth into the crevices until it could be smoothed off and whitewashed. The floor was made from locally produced bricks and the roof of asbestos, which the children would turn the sprinkler onto, to try to keep it cool on hot days.

The roof beams were painted with creosote to deter borer worms but there was not much to be done about termites, which periodically ate away the poles inside the walls so that they had to be replaced. The boys remember vividly the time they were unable to move the sofa because it had been cemented to the floor by termites, which also succeeded in permanently sealing one of the drawers of Nigel's roll-top desk. It became a standing joke among their neighbours that Nigel and Corona still lived in a 'pole and daga' house long after their farm workers had brick ones. The incongruity was further emphasised by the oil portraits of Thornycroft and Gurney ancestors and the paintings, books, silver, china and fine furniture with which they filled it.

The plan was for a proper brick house with a thatched roof to replace it within three years or so, but it was long in coming. First of all the money they set aside for the project was embezzled, although neither of them ever referred to that again, and then, just as they felt secure enough financially to start building, there came a series of disastrous tobacco harvests from 1961-1963 and then the war. The new house was eventually built in 1980 on a lovely and long-planned site overlooking the dam built by Frank Scott in 1952 when he still owned Sheffield.

Scott's Dam was almost two miles long and could be used to irrigate the tobacco lands, making possible a second crop a year. Opposite the site of the new house, there were tall reed beds, in which egrets roosted and weaver birds nested, and much of the water was covered by water-lilies, until, in the dry years, so much water was pumped out onto the tobacco lands that bush pig were able to get at the water-lily bulbs. Nigel and Corona ate breakfast every day in the bay window overlooking the dam, with a pair of binoculars on the windowsill, and had tea every afternoon on the verandah that had the same view.

The dam attracted Googly, a hippopotamus that came over the dam wall from Numwa, usually on its own but occasionally with others. It would play hide and seek with the dogs, allowing them to swim out and almost reach it before sinking out of sight, only to re-emerge a few minutes later some way off for the whole diverting game to start again. It would also follow Corona's canoe while she was fishing for bream. It was not welcome in the garden and Corona once used her beloved .410 to pepper it and a companion, knowing that the shot would not penetrate their thick hides but hoping that the sting would deter them. She claimed afterwards to be the only woman in Africa to have shot a right and left of hippo.

But that all seemed a long way in the future when Corona began to set up home in the original house at Merryhill. She had help to cook, clean and wash clothes and the redoubtable Mrs David, whose husband managed the labour on the farm for Nigel for fifteen years, to see that everything ran smoothly. Mrs David also looked after the children. Hugh (universally known as Dillo) was born in the Mundell's barn on 3rd March 1950 and Richard in the 'pole and daga' house on 24th April 1952. Mrs David would pick them up and sling them on her back, when she felt they were getting under Corona's feet.

With five hungry boys to feed, Corona employed a gardener to grow vegetables and fruit, including 'naartjies' (mandarin oranges), lemons and plums. From her neighbour Ruth Gebbie, Corona learnt how to keep, and pluck, chickens. She also kept a cow for milk. For many years the gardener was a man called Reedy. He could not always resist the temptation to sell milk and other produce for his own benefit and was periodically banished to work on the tobacco lands but Corona needed him in the garden and he always came back. The boys set great store by his ability to make models of farm animals from the clay that became available whenever a dam was being built, of which they built up herds. For Reedy, any time spent making clay cows was time saved from more arduous duties. Nevertheless,

Corona's gardens became a delight and the scent of roses was a consistent memory of Merryhill for many guests. They installed electricity after a year or so. The ability to keep food cool made a huge difference but one never knew, on looking into the freezer, whether one would be greeted by food for the family, rations for the staff, meat for the dogs or a snake or some other creature waiting to be dissected by one of the boys. The loos, originally 'long-drops', one of which Mike had to descend on a rope to rescue an idiotic hen that had fallen in, were also replaced with flushing systems.

Nigel's aim was to build up a mixed economy farm that he could hand on to his sons. That included cattle, and they need water. Over the years, Nigel built twenty three dams. They were usually only an acre or two in extent, named for friends and family, as in Dillo's Dam or Richard's Dam, and held water for about eight months of the year. As they dried out they provided attractive feeding places for wild duck that felt safer from predators out on the wet mud that fringed the receding water than on what had been dry banks.

Roads had to be built too. Nigel had them carefully surveyed but was, as ever, closely involved in the 'hands-on' work. There was a boulder that had to be moved if he was to complete Broom's Bridge (named for one of the Merryhill assistants). It could not be dug out, so he put dynamite under it while the farm workers and his children watched from a place of safety. The rock rose majestically to a height of about six feet before subsiding back into its hole. He tried again, using twenty sticks of dynamite, and staff and children watched in awe from behind anthills as exactly the same thing happened, although the rock reached a height of about twenty feet this time. Not to be beaten, Nigel placed a whole box, which consisted of fifty sticks, underneath the rock. This time the eighty-ton boulder and its accompanying debris flew past Nigel and over the heads of the watching staff and children to land on the far side of his parked car.

As soon as he could, Nigel spent £300 on twenty Hereford cows, and later bought a pedigree Hereford bull. The white faces of the Herefords made them susceptible to sunburn and eye infections, so he developed a Hereford-Afrikaner cross that suited the country better and about which he cared passionately. His cattleman, Sylvester, cared too and his gap-toothed grin was infectious whenever he and

Nigel succeeded in rescuing a cow that was mired in the thick black mud that surrounded a shrinking dam or in wrestling out a calf that was having a difficult birth (at least once by tying it to the back of the Renault and pulling it out by horsepower). No matter how close to death a cow was, Nigel would attempt to nurse it back to health, lifting it to its feet, walking it round and hand-feeding it three times a day.

Nigel insisted on the cattle being treated with respect, and the over-use of sticks, shouting or twisting their tails made him furious. His herd was calm and comparatively easy to manage as a result. Between 1963 and 1969 he installed a system of multiple paddocks that could be grazed at high density for short periods followed by a long rest for the grass to recover before it was needed again. By 1969 Nigel had six hundred and fifty head grazing forty paddocks and he eventually built up the herd to eight hundred.

He would trust no-one but himself to dehorn or castrate the calves, even in later years when he would take two or three days to recover from the physical demands of a dehorning session. He kept a legendarily sharp knife for the purpose, honed for hours on an oilstone but seldom cleaned except by a wipe on the seat of his shorts. You did not really want him to cut you a slice of 'biltong' after lancing one of the abscesses, caused by ticks, which the cows suffered from.

His friend and neighbour, David Hamilton, regarded Nigel as an effective, hard-working and successful farmer although loss of so much money in that unfortunate

investment meant that he could never be in the top bracket. He was also undeniably accident prone. He lost the tip of a finger to a cut that went septic. He took to wearing a monocle after a tennis ball hit him in the eye.

On holiday on the coast of Mozambique, he slipped a disc lunging for a fishing rod that had been taken by something big. He was quite unable to move and in great pain so Dillo, with the help of local fishermen, had to make a stretcher from casuarina (ironwood) poles they found on the beach, carry him to a boat, row it across the lagoon and pack Nigel into the vehicle for a six hour drive along bad roads back to Rhodesia and an operation. The only available anaesthetic for the agonising journey was two bottles of Portuguese brandy bought from a roadside store, which Nigel quickly and gratefully consumed. He very nearly died from coral poisoning after another holiday on the Mozambique coast and would almost certainly have done so had a neighbour not made Corona take him to a doctor. Her usual response to these events was a resigned *"Oh dear, what a bore!"*

David Hamilton had immense respect for Nigel's conservation and habitat protection work. His ideas, and especially his tree planting programme, were well ahead of his time and his dedication to conservation was recognised by the award of a Natural Resources Board Certificate of Merit in 1980. Nigel sat on the committee of the South Marandellas (now Marondera) Intensive Conservation Area (ICA) for many years and was Chairman from 1958. Corona did a long stint as Secretary. She and Nigel worked hard to get farmers in the neighbouring Tribal Trust Lands to accept the benefits of long term planning and of conserving the soil, trees, wildlife and grazing by showing African farmers round the commercial farms and encouraging them to copy those practices that were viable for them.

Nigel did a series of radio interviews to spread the conservation message. He wrote, and Corona illustrated, regular articles for 'The

Wedza Farmers' Gazette' and 'The Field' back in England about the wildlife on their farm. When Sir Peter Scott, as he was by then, came out to Zimbabwe to do a radio programme about conservation, Nigel and Corona were invited to join him and Lady Scott for a few days on Lake Kariba.

Because of his wide knowledge of the bush and its wildlife, Nigel was asked in 1971 to act as a courier for Abercrombie and Kent, which catered for small, select and personalised groups of tourists. When Nigel collected his first party, headed by an American senator, from Salisbury (now Harare) Airport, he was completely stumped by the very first question *"What is the population of Rhodesia?"* The best Nigel could do in response was *"Well, the telephone directory is about this thick"*, measuring about half an inch between finger and thumb. The senator was delighted and not only returned for several more trips, insisting on having Nigel as his courier, but had Nigel and Corona out to stay on his cattle ranch in 1983. During the trip, Nigel caught a sturgeon that broke the record for the Idaho River.

Nigel was keen to preserve as much of the 'msasa' and 'munondo' woods on Merryhill as he could. He also planted pines and gum trees to provide him with windbreaks, shade, timber, fuel and a surplus to sell. It may have been the tree planting, or his insistence that every stick of tobacco was filled to capacity, or simply his long, lean figure that gave him his Shona name of *"Kamtepi"*, meaning stick.

Nigel was certainly an unmistakable figure in his monocle, frayed jersey, and khaki shorts, well hitched up to reveal long, brown and usually rather scratched and battered legs. Unlike his five sons, who were all supremely competent, he was completely uninterested in things mechanical. He drove a maroon Renault 4, one of the few cars available in Zimbabwe that could accommodate his height, which he referred to as a *"sewing machine on wheels"*. He removed the back seat in order to create more room for wire strainers, tick grease and so on and there is a story that he once stopped for a hitch-hiker who took one look and declined the lift. He used to get it up to fourth gear and keep it there whatever the road conditions and, as he grew older and his neck grew stiff, he perfected a reversing technique of simply going backwards until he hit something.

During the lean times, Nigel wrote a little poem in the style of A P Herbert that began:

"The farmer will never be happy again;
He carries his heart in his boots;
For either the dry is destroying his gwaai (tobacco)
Or the wet is destroying his roots.

"You may speak, if you can, to this querulous man,
Though I should not attempt to be funny,
And if you insist he will give you a list
Of the reasons he's making no money."

In fact, it was only the proceeds from Corona's various ventures that financed the five boys through school, and kept the farm going through the hard times.

CHAPTER 7

BRINGING UP THE FAMILY

Sitting room from dining table end.
Merryhill

At first, Corona was as busy as any farmer's wife, bringing up a family, running the household and looking after the interests of the farm workers' families, and she had little leisure to develop her own interests. While money was tight, she made most of the boys' school clothes, which meant six white shirts, six khaki shirts and six pairs of shorts for each of them, some seventy items. Even with the ability to pass clothes on from a bigger to a smaller brother, the sewing on of new name tapes seemed a never ending task. She made most of her own clothes, and cushions and curtains for the house, as well as knitting all Nigel's jerseys.

She walked every day, at about four in the afternoon for an hour, with the dogs away out in front, and the children trailing behind. On the way home the order would be reversed with the children racing home and the weary dogs bringing up the rear. The dogs began with a line of Pekingese: Winkle, a great character and an excellent ratter who would sit up on her hindquarters begging for a piece of Nigel's bacon through the whole of breakfast; Missee Lee, named after the Chinese pirate in Arthur Ransome's book of the same name; Chuff and Chuff Two. Other dogs of various breeds followed, including terriers called Biscuit and Milo.

Nigel's dogs were all liver and white Springer spaniels, apart from Pip's Labrador Mudge, whom Nigel took on when Pip and his family went to Canada. They were less imaginatively named, being alternately Bill and Bob. For some reason the Bills normally turned out to be better shooting dogs than the Bobs. Dillo still remembers the awful, silent breakfast to which Nigel brought a .45 pistol before carrying his beloved Bill, only 9 years old but paralysed, out to the gum trees to put him out of his suffering and bury him.

From time to time one of the cats, like Kitty Mytton, the big Siamese, or Piwi, a hand-reared serval (a beautifully spotted species of African wild cat) would come on the walks too. The fastidious Piwi used to use the loo by the bothy, leaving a neat pile of cigar shaped droppings in one corner.

Once there were five boys, their bedroom became overcrowded. The original hen house was converted into an extra bedroom, always known as the bothy, in which the younger boys slept and which they loved. It was a hundred yards from the house. The windows were near the ground and were the preferred means of entry and exit. It was a good place for telling ghost stories, and when Richard's brothers left for school and he had to sleep there alone, he spent some wakeful nights.

Corona always said that Nigel was better with the children than she was, and her sons admit that her mothering skills were limited. She could be impatient. Taking the boys to fish on the spillway at Scott's Dam involved shooting a dove to use as bait with the .22 rifle on the way down. On one occasion, Mike missed a bird, handed the rifle to Pip, who also missed, as did Dillo. Exclaiming *"Oh, give it to me!"* Corona knocked the bird out of the tree with her first shot. In contrast, Nigel actively enjoyed the boys' company and encouraged their interest in what he was doing and why, but even he did not always remember to bring as many home as he had started out with when they accompanied him on his farm rounds.

Like many people, they may have found grandchildren easier. Pip's son Justin recalls painting with Corona in what he describes as long, companionable silences and Richard's children, who called her 'umbuya' (Shona for granny), remember walking the farm with her, looking for pottery and identifying which tribe had made it and when. Rosanne remembers well her unusual birthday present of 5 kilograms of bird seed, which she fed enthusiastically to the Egyptian geese on the lawn. Nigel had a special soothing whistle, the same one that he used on his cows, with which he communicated with his smaller grandchildren.

Both Nigel and Corona were well read. Corona believed that she had read every single large print book in the Marondera, and later the Borradaile, library. The boys were encouraged to do the same, and books by Enid Blyton, W J Long, and Rudyard Kipling were read aloud to them.

They played board games, Scrabble or Patience. Television came into their lives much later and was only really used for Test cricket and wildlife or National Geographic documentaries, although Nigel daily listened to the radio news on the BBC World Service.

The boys describe their growing up as fierce but free. Manners, politeness and respect for others were certainly fiercely enforced. From the age of ten they had to change into long trousers and a tie to join Nigel and Corona in the dining room, instead of having supper earlier on their own. Nigel would enjoy a brandy and soda, and Corona a brandy and water or a gin and tonic, before Nigel ordered dinner to be brought in. The household was not as unfailingly smoothly run as that image might suggest. On the occasion that he ordered a *"pot of tea"* from a member of staff new to the household, there was a long delay until he was presented with a 5 litre container of hot water with a tea bag floating in it.

When they went out, for example to birthday parties held by other children, the four younger boys would be well turned out in white shirts, ties, shorts, stockings and shoes. Their usual practice was to descend on the tea table at once before taking off to the nearest koppie to organise games that were rather less tame than the 'ring of roses' or 'round the mulberry bush' being laid on by their hostess. If they were still absent when the time came to leave, Corona would simply ask anyone passing the turning to Merryhill to drop them off later.

Nigel laid down strict rules where firearms were concerned. The boys were given access to an airgun on their tenth birthdays but it could only be used under Nigel's supervision for the first year. However, he was careful to set aside time to educate them in the rules and etiquette of shooting, not least respect for the quarry. When Pip shot a small bird that was not regarded as legitimate quarry one Christmas, it was plucked, roasted and solemnly brought in to the dining room alongside the turkey. Nigel made him eat it before he could have anything else. It was a lesson all the boys took to heart.

Once they were eleven they were free to take the gun out on their own, although Nigel decreed that it could only be taken out by one boy at a time to minimise the risk of an accident. When the inevitable happened and a ricochet lodged in Richard's toe, no-one betrayed the infringement of the rule and the wound festered for days until an X-ray revealed the incriminating truth. At eleven they were also allowed to join shoots on the farm as Guns, using their mother's .410, instead of as beaters. At twelve they graduated to a 12-bore shotgun and had the freedom of the farm to shoot vermin, mainly pigs or monkeys, if their numbers were getting out of hand.

Only one boy at a time was allowed to use The Blue Gnu, a small collapsible canvas canoe. Nigel was once extremely angry to see three boys and the canoe on an island in the middle of a treacherous stretch of the Zambezi until they were able show him the ingenious system of rope and fishing line that had enabled them to pull the empty canoe back to the home bank between trips.

Other rules included only being allowed two ingredients on any sandwich, which taught the virtues of moderation as well as being economical. But where there were no rules, the boys had the freedom of the whole farm and were positively encouraged to use it and to learn from their mistakes. If they elected not to wear shoes and picked up a splinter, there was no cause for complaint or need for sympathy.

From an early age, they clamoured to be allowed to sleep outside. At first they tended to scuttle back indoors when it got really dark, but they were soon making businesslike camps in the bush. Once the four younger boys waited all night armed with 'pangas' (machetes) by the hole of a porcupine that was raiding the kitchen garden. Perhaps luckily, they all fell asleep before it ventured out. When Dillo went to visit the Hamiltons one afternoon and stayed for four days, Corona is alleged to have said, on meeting Pat Hamilton in the village, *"Oh, so that is where he's been"*. Pip, aged fifteen, bicycled up to Lusaka in Zambia alone, sleeping under a bridge one night when he could find no other accommodation. Richard, at about the same age, bicycled down to Durban in South Africa with a friend, a feat that was reported in the local paper.

There were dangers in such freedom. Mike came close to electrocuting himself one Christmas. Pip almost died from not being diagnosed with trypanosomiasis (sleeping sickness) in time after he, Mike and Dillo had been infected by tsetse flies while down the Valley. Richard accidentally spilt a tin of petrol over himself while playing in the boiler room and caught fire. He too almost died. Corona offered to buy him a teddy bear as a reward for his bravery after two weeks in hospital undergoing painful skin grafts but he declined on the grounds that his elder brothers would laugh at him.

It was after this crisis, during which the support of the local Catholic priest had been a great comfort, that Corona began to think seriously about converting to Catholicism. She agonised for weeks about what she felt would be a dagger through her marriage but, when she plucked up the courage to tell Nigel, he simply responded *"Damn! Then I shall have to become a Catholic too."*

Outside the farm and the family, the heart of the community lay in the Wedza Country Club. The Clubhouse was built by (or with materials contributed by) the farmers and their families. The bar was run by the husbands and the catering was done by their wives in rotation. The combination of Corona and Pat Hamilton on the roster one year was generally acknowledged afterwards to be a mistake since neither was remotely domestic, although Corona did make good sandwiches. After one dinner cooked by Corona, the smell of roasting porcupine meat lingered in the Clubhouse kitchen for days.

The Club provided golf, cricket, tennis, film shows, swimming and plays, in which Corona, her sons and their wives and even Nigel on occasion took part. Corona took the lead role of Mrs Branson in Evelyn Williams' 'Night Must Fall', the first ever production of the Wedza Players. She revelled in a neighbour's tribute that she had *"the best legs in Wedza"*. Farmers' meetings, the annual Wedza Tobacco Show, birthday parties, Christmas parties, including the one organised every year for the children by Mike Hill, and a formal New Year's Eve dance at which the men wore black tie and the women long dresses were all held at the Club.

Nigel habitually looked, in David Hamilton's words, *"as though he had just come from a wrestling match with his cattle"*, but he and Corona were a most striking couple when they did take the trouble to dress up. Nigel was tall, good looking and had perfect manners, and Corona, also tall, had real dignity and superb features. Evening dress was commonly worn at dinner parties, and hats and gloves to go into town, when they first arrived, but things were less formal than in England. Corona was relieved to be able to throw away her whalebone corsets, although she was rather startled when the cook appropriated them and wore them to serve dinner one night.

Nigel was an enthusiastic stalwart of the Club cricket team. He was a slow off-spin bowler, who headed the bowling averages at Wedza until he retired from the game in 1977, aged sixty seven. He was not such a successful batsman but he was an intimidating fielder at gully, walking forward as the bowler came in, with his hands held wide and ready for a catch. The spectacle reminded his team-mates of a heron stalking an unsuspecting fish and they christened him 'Stalky'.

In June 1982 the Wedza Club was invited to send a team to England for a series of village cricket games. The final match of the tour was against The Gentlemen of Shropshire, a side that had been run for years by Nigel's brother Guy, just as the Hereford Gents had been run by their father. Nigel, then aged seventy two, came out of retirement and flew over to play in it. Unfortunately, he had been severely kicked the day before by a cow he was attempting to dip and his bruises had been liberally painted in gentian violet by Corona, to the amusement of his team-mates and the ill-concealed astonishment of their opponents.

He served as Chairman of the cricket team until his death, when Corona was elected to succeed him. She was still Chairman when the team was disbanded in 2002 on the wholesale eviction of the Wedza farmers. Nigel also occasionally captained it, taking a keen pleasure in good performances by other and especially younger players, just as his father had done. There were times when there were even more Thornycrofts on the Wedza Club team list than the Hereford Gents had been able to muster.

Corona taught all the boys at home for two years before they went off to boarding school at St Michael's Prep School and then St George's College in Salisbury. St George's, with all the constraints imposed by the Jesuits who ran it, was not a success and when an opportunity arose they took all the boys away. They sent them to Umtali High School, which suited them much better. As it happened, Robin was by then working for Central African Petroleum Refineries (CAPREF) in Umtali and the boys were able to board with him and his new bride, which cannot have been easy for her. Nigel provided them with an old car to get them to school. They quickly learnt how to maintain it themselves, and made a habit of free-wheeling down every hill to make their petrol allowance go further.

While the boys were away at school, their parents did not come to watch matches or visit them, as it was widely believed to be unsettling, although later they did go to watch their grandchildren's matches. On the other hand when Pip, unjustly accused of theft, or Dillo, bored and intending to live in the bush, ran away from school, Nigel listened to them patiently and talked to them wisely until they decided for themselves that the right thing to do would be to go back. The converse of this 'hands-off' approach was that the holidays were for the boys. Nigel and Corona would set aside all except essential work to plan sporting and other activities and expeditions to Kariba or to fish the Gairezi. Dillo recalls that *"Our childhood was filled to the brim with adventure"*.

Nigel wrote to each of the five boys once a fortnight and Corona wrote every week for the whole of their boarding school life. Nigel also wrote regularly afterwards, spending an hour at his roll-top desk after breakfast almost every day, dispensing forthright, and usually unsolicited, advice about money, jobs and bringing up children. He would break off to report that *"five wood ibis have just dropped in to the mud flash below"* and interrupt himself again a few lines later to exclaim *"bloody old fish eagle has just pushed the ibis off, rot him"*. A combination of paper shortages, brought about by economic sanctions during the war, and Nigel's clumsiness meant that a number of his surviving letters were sent despite having had ink or tea spilt on them, or even been set on fire.

They may not have given them an entirely conventional upbringing, but Nigel and Corona were well satisfied with the good manners, self-reliance and easy confidence that characterised their sons in later life.

CHAPTER 8
DOWN THE VALLEY

'Jellyfish.'

Given the demands of farm and family, it was three years before Corona and Nigel felt able to take a holiday. They went to a totally unsuitable beach hotel in South Africa, full of rich Johannesburg people. The next year, and for years after that, they went to Paradise Island off the Mozambique coast with the Travers and Hamilton families. They used to fly down in a double winged de Havilland Rapide belonging to Jack Malloch, in whose transport business Mike later became a pilot. They would hire a boat and set up camp near the well of a ruined Portuguese fort on the island. There was a reef and the clear water offered superb goggling. Nigel had a series of crayfishing spears made up from broom handles with sharpened metal tips added by the local engineering shop before he left. These were deemed too dangerous for the children, but they had plenty to do, including goggling, taking the boat out for dorado, marlin or sailfish and fly fishing for garfish.

David Hamilton remembers how he and Pat joined Nigel and Corona for a few days on the neighbouring island of Bazaruto. Having hitched a lift on a boat, they were dropped off with a couple of demi-johns of water and some bread, confident that they could catch enough fish, crab and crayfish. However, when the time came to eat, it transpired that Corona had forgotten to bring any cutlery. *"Oh well"* said Nigel *"we'll have to use shells and sticks"* and they duly set off to gather some. At bedtime, Corona found that she had forgotten blankets and had to borrow one from Pat. In the morning, Nigel discovered he had forgotten his bathing trunks. Apologizing to Pat that *"they are a little revealing. You won't mind, will you?"* he put on a pair of Dillo's pyjamas. By the end of the trip, they were split from front to back into two virtually separate pieces. Paradise Island was somewhere they never tired of, until holiday cottages, then a hotel and finally an airstrip took away the magic and they stopped going.

Fishing camps followed as the boys grew bigger. The Pungwe River rises in the Eastern Highlands, where there is always rain, and they used to fly fish its upper reaches in Inyanga. The river then makes its way through Mozambique to the coast. Some forty yards wide and three feet deep, it is fast flowing and gin clear, with huge pools that are hard to wade. A trip to fish the Pungwe in its middle reaches near Gorangoza involved a long drive, being ferried across the river and then cutting a way through anything up to ten miles of bush to set up camp on the river bank. Fresh water prawns could be caught by simply leaving a leafy branch in the water overnight and yanking it out briskly in the morning with the prawns that had sought sanctuary in it still there. They were used for bait to catch bream and tigerfish.

Nigel and Dillo once took an unlicensed camping trip in Nigel's Renault to fish the Pungwe in Inyanga. On the way they had an accident that smashed the windscreen of the car, which they parked up in the bush on the river bank. When Corona received a phone call from the police to say that they had found the damaged and apparently abandoned car she was unsure at first whether to be more worried that they had been hurt or that she would get them in trouble for poaching by admitting where they were and what they were doing.

The Gairezi is a tributary of the Pungwe. It was stocked with rainbow trout by a Club that imposed strict bag limits, but extra fish were allowed to anyone who took out eels and Nigel and Corona and the boys often took advantage of that concession. Nigel was a good fisherman but he regarded it as an activity best enjoyed alone. On one occasion, leaving Corona to fish one pool, he came across Pat Hamilton fishing another and turned away without a word. Further upstream he bumped into David Hamilton, who asked him if he had had any luck. Nigel exploded *"Perish the thought, David, the bloody place is like Brighton Beach on a Bank Holiday"* before moving on again. At the time they were the only four people on five kilometres of river.

After the dam across the Zambezi at Kariba was completed in 1958, a huge lake over two hundred miles long gradually formed behind it. Nigel and his neighbour Tony Seager were among the volunteers who manned boats to rescue over six thousand large animals and countless smaller ones that were cut off and condemned to drown on shrinking islands. It was wild and lovely country and both the game viewing and the fishing were spectacular. Nigel regularly took his family there on fishing camps, staying on Redcliff Island. On one trip he caught a 25 lb tigerfish that was briefly a Rhodesian record. It was mounted and long held pride of place over the bar of the Wedza Club, where it occasionally suffered from being used as a target during the war when farmers took their weapons everywhere with them, including into the bar.

The greatest sporting highlight of most years was a ten day hunting camp in the Zambezi River Valley, for which members of the National Hunters' Association could bid. The camps, several thousand acres of bush, and a specific number of animals of various kinds were allocated by lottery. Each of the boys in turn became a member of the Hunters' Association, which increased their chances of getting a camp, as did the extra chance afforded to anyone prepared to instruct at the Conservation Education camp for teenagers at Rifa, as Mike and Richard both did.

The boys were taken on these camps from the age of fourteen, having experienced fishing camps at Kariba from eleven or twelve. They still remember the eager anticipation that came with packing. It could be pretty haphazard unless the methodical Mike took over the loading of the vehicle. Corona laughed out loud at her sister-in-law Puss' horror on discovering that several items of Thornycroft silver and china had been put aside to take down the Valley. The excitement mounted during the long drive until they reached the top of the escarpment and looked down into the Zambezi Valley below them, completely wild because tsetse fly meant that no cattle could live there. It was hot, flat and dry, with the great river that had created it still invisible under 'mopane' trees and the occasional, gigantic baobab. They had to book in with the Parks Board at Marangora, where the warning photograph on the wall showing what tsetse fly bites looked like was of Dillo's leg. Finally, there came the long, dusty drive down terrible roads into camp. 'A' Camp was the highest up the river, by the Gorge where semi-precious stones formed the pebbles on the river bed. Their favourite was 'B' Camp, further down towards Chirundu in a grove of kapok and African mahogany, where the river widened out, clean, fast flowing, and clear enough to see the fish in.

The temptation to get into or onto the river as soon as they arrived was almost unbearable but unpacking the bedrolls, Tilley lamps, charcoal filter fridge and the pump for getting water up from the river had to come first. Wood for the camp fires and drying racks had to be collected and stacked. Only then could the canoes be taken down from the roof of the vehicle and launched.

In the years before the Kariba dam was built and the river tamed, the water levels used to go up and down dramatically. Sometimes fish would be cut off in shrinking pools so that the boys could chase and catch them with their hands. Sometimes the river was so full the only way to catch fish was with goggles and a spear. Nigel described the procedure in a letter to Robin *"my 'job' was to keep 10 yards behind a goggler in the canoe with instructions if croc or hippo appeared a) to beat on the canoe - presumably to alert the goggler - b) do the same on the hippo or croc & c) embark the intrepid goggler - or what was left of him - and return to camp. If you've ever tried to keep 10 yards behind a goggler ...when your target is either paddling swiftly ahead, stopping suddenly, or shooting off underwater - well, my money would have been firmly on croc or hippo. In fact we met neither."*

88

Once, Pip caught an electric catfish. As he touched the metal trace, he got an electric shock. He called Mike over and persuaded him to pick it up, with the same happy result.

They managed to play the trick successfully on Dillo before the three of them gleefully took it back to camp to see if they could catch Nigel out. They should have known better.

The party normally consisted of four hunters and six or so staff, some to help with running the camp and some Game and Wildlife Department employees who acted as trackers and ensured that the bag limits were strictly adhered to. The Merryhill farm staff were brought on the trip as a reward for good work. It was a much cherished opportunity to eat fresh meat. One year, when the time came to leave, Nigel made all the staff take their suitcases down from the vehicle and open them. Each one contained almost nothing but 'biltong' (strips of dried meat). When he was asked what had made him suspicious, Nigel pointed out that despite the sultry heat of the valley, each of them was wearing several shirts, a jersey and practically every other item of clothing he possessed.

Nigel reminded Robin why he found it all so exciting in a letter that described the pre-dawn drive along the river to find the tracks of animals that had come down to drink during the night. Then the hunter, accompanied by one or, on this occasion, two trackers, would abandon the vehicle and set out on foot to follow the trail. *Usually the first two or three miles among the little hills from the river were largely gravel, rock and very thin grass and how they held the line beats me all ends up. Back in the thick cover there was more soil and sometimes it seemed easier, while in the myriad acres of jesse* (scrub), *access was limited to game trails - a twisting convoluted multitude thereof that would have put Hampton Court Maze to shame. This was the most thrilling part, for often you couldn't see ten yards, and the number of fallen trees and patches of black shadow that froze you dead in your tracks for heart thumping minutes were legion. And eventually there*

had to be that twitch of ear or tail or curving gleam of horn. Or the almost unbearable crash and thump of stampede as the beasties got your wind and all was over."

At the end of the long, hot day, everybody would return to camp to swap stories of their successes and failures round a blazing fire of 'mopane' wood. It was a part of the day that Nigel loved, particularly later when he stopped hunting himself and spent his days watching birds and walking with Corona while she sketched or looked for plants. Not that they slowed down completely. He told Robin of a *"short paddle"* they took from the Gorge back to camp in the canoes when they were both in their seventies. It was over twelve miles.

Anything they did not eat was made into 'biltong' for future hunts or taken back as farm rations. It was a point of honour that no meat should be wasted. The drying meat, of course, acted as a magnet to hyenas, and sometimes lion or leopard, and the fire was kept going all night under the chicken-wire drying racks to try to prevent too much from being stolen as well as to keep away flies. If animals did raid the drying meat, the Parks Board trackers were adamant that they could not be shot unless they were on the license. The baboon that regularly stole meat on one camp was therefore safe, until the morning he became foolhardy enough to take mealie meal from the trackers' own rations.

Their early camps were organised by Gerry von Memerty, who Nigel described in 1982, after they had got back from an unarmed stalk that had taken them right into the middle of a herd of elephants, as *"an absolute genius with elephant - they are one of his passions in life - and an utter joy to be with alone in the bush, and nowadays, like me, rather un-bloodthirsty apart from food."* Gerry was almost killed when a lion came through the camp unseen one night, passing twenty yards from Nigel, as the tracks made clear in the morning, but pausing by Gerry's bed to rake his face with its claws, apparently startled by his snores. They patched him up as best they could and drove him for four hours to Kariba. He was then sedated so that he could be taken the 350 miles to Salisbury where he had sixty six stitches.

Tragically, he was killed on a camp in 1990 when he found himself in the middle of a herd of elephant cows and their calves in thick bush. The herd became very agitated and when his companion lost sight of him he returned to camp to alert Corona and her sons. Robin, Mike, Dillo and Richard were all there and it was they who found his body, after hours of searching, and deduced what had happened from the tracks. Gerry was behind a tree hiding from an elephant to his front when he was run through from behind by another. His rifle lay beside him, unfired.

Corona did not go on the early expeditions but, once she did, she too fell in love with the swift and turbulent river, with its hippo, tigerfish, 'vundu' (giant barbel), and bream. She used to take long walks on her own while the men were out hunting, like the day on which she found an Egyptian goose's nest while crawling through the sand to try to get close to a hippo. Fearing that the eggs were bound to be trampled by their huge neighbours, she took them back to camp with a view to hatching them. Surprisingly, the job of keeping them warm for the week until their return to Merryhill (and the services of a broody hen), fell to Nigel, who took them into his sleeping bag every night. Two of them, appropriately named Anthony and Cleopatra, survived to found the dynasty of Egyptian geese that subsequently colonised the Wedza area. On another camp an elephant tried to pass between the sleeping forms of Nigel and Corona but, finding there was no room, backed quietly away. They found the tracks in the morning and Nigel was furious to have slept through it.

After the occasion on which they were nearly killed by a buffalo, she would never have dreamed of going out without a companion armed with a rifle. It happened while Nigel and Corona were shooting guinea fowl, out of sight of the rest of the party. Corona had shot one guinea fowl when she saw the buffalo. She called out to Nigel, who was temporarily invisible in a patch of 'jesse', a tangle of twelve foot high shrubs and trees, threaded through by trails that were almost tunnels that allowed the game to move. To her horror, the buffalo charged into the 'jesse' and Corona heard grunting and snorting. She ran in to find Nigel on his back with his long legs wrapped around the animal's neck, holding grimly on to its horns while it battered him against the ground. Corona stepped up to it and, putting the muzzle of her shotgun against where she hoped its heart was, shot it with both barrels. Buffalo do not pay much heed to the sort of pellets designed for guinea fowl and she was appalled when, after rolling briefly onto its side, it returned to the business of killing her husband.

But the momentary respite had allowed Nigel to scramble to his feet and recover enough breath to shout "Give me the bloody gun!" his own being somewhere underneath the buffalo. Nigel seldom swore in earnest. He shot it again, knocking it back on its haunches. He just had time to reload before the beast attacked again. Fearing he would run out of cartridges, he shot it in the eyes and then the nose, to make sure it could not follow them if they had to make a run for it. As its rushes became weaker he was able to shoot it repeatedly, until it finally rolled onto its side and died. Nigel was remarkably little hurt apart from a bloody gash down one shin and two broken ribs. He collected his gun and they not only walked back to the vehicle but shot another guinea fowl on the way. Nevertheless once the reaction set in, Corona remembered afterwards, he had some difficulty in picking up his sun-downer without spilling it that night.

They arrived back at the vehicle to find the others had thought, from the number of shots they had heard, that they had been having excellent sport. There was general disbelief when they said that they had shot a buffalo, and even when they persuaded them that they were telling the truth, their main concern was that Nigel had no license to kill a buffalo. A trip to Marangora to buy a retrospective license was the immediate priority. Gradually the full story came out and their astonishing coolness, presence of mind, sheer courage and luck in a situation which could well have resulted in death for one or both of them became the stuff of legend.

Nigel was not a vindictive man but a dice box made from the buffalo's scrotum stood on the mantelpiece at Merryhill ever afterwards.

CHAPTER 9

AT WAR AGAIN

War had not yet done with Nigel and Corona. Rhodesia made a Unilateral Declaration of Independence from Britain on 11th November 1965, in order to avoid being forced into granting majority rule before she was ready to do so. Britain did nothing about it, except to impose economic sanctions on the infant country. Sanctions were pretty ineffectual at first, simply serving to encourage farmers to diversify into those crops that could no longer be imported. However, with international markets closed, Nigel admitted in 1978 that *"though one laughs at them, (sanctions) have in fact cut most farm incomes to subsistence or debt"*.

Merryhill was no exception, and might have gone under like so many others had it not been for Corona's determination, business acumen and artistic talent. To help pay the bills, she began to make, and sell, Christmas cards out of pressed grasses and everlasting flowers. They sold well and she was asked to make little framed pictures too, then bigger pictures, calendars and fire screens. The discovery that she could make attractive and realistic birds from feathers made her work inimitable by competitors who had neither her knowledge of birds nor her artistic skill. Her speciality was guinea fowl, standing, flying or running, made from real guinea fowl feathers and given life by a few deft pen strokes to delineate head and legs, and instantly recognisable as her work. In order to maximise her profits by cutting out the middleman, she took the brave decision to go it alone. That meant that she had to find reliable, wholesale quantities of suitable card, glue and dye and be responsible for her own marketing, a time consuming job which she was thrilled to be able to delegate, at least partly, to Robin's son Adrian, who proved rather good at it.

Growing success allowed her to take on six local women, training them to cut the washed and softened feathers into shapes carefully copied from Corona's bird book. They worked in the bothy that had progressed from hen house to boys' dormitory and now to a whitewashed workshop with trestle tables and chairs running down the middle. At the height of her business she was selling more than fifteen thousand pressed flower pictures and greetings cards a year at Barber's department store in Salisbury and exporting them to South Africa and beyond. In her best year she turned over a very respectable $17,000 and was able to buy two prefabricated houses, one as a workshop and one for the women to sleep in. Nigel was immensely proud of her success, and, once he had handed over the running of the farm to Dillo and eventually Richard, he became what he called *"framer-in-chief"*.

Since Britain did not intervene, the African nationalist parties left Rhodesia to start a war of terror from outside the country, infiltrating in small numbers to attempt to win over the people and then to attack white farmers when they felt strong enough. Corona estimated that about three quarters of the Wedza farm workers helped the guerrillas with information or food and shelter, although there was no way of knowing how much was by coercion and how much out of sympathy for their cause. Nigel and Corona were not the least interested in the politics but, once a shooting war began, they were in no doubt that, once again, they would have to do their bit.

Most of the older farmers joined the Police Reserve and were regularly called out for two weeks service at a time. Many of them were used to escort the daily convoys bringing small arms, ammunition, oil and other vital supplies up the road from South Africa under the constant threat of ambush. Corona sympathised with the wives left behind to cope on their own, but could not help remembering that she had been left on her own for almost six years the last time.

The younger men served mostly in the part-time Rhodesian Regiment. The commitment gradually increased until anyone less than 38 years old had to undertake twelve month's initial military service followed by a recall of one month out of every three. This was very disruptive to the farming cycle and it was realised that it made more sense to keep farmers in their own area to fight in and for their own communities. Many left the Army to join their local paramilitary Police Anti-Terrorist Unit (PATU) instead.

All four of the younger boys were involved and all four saw active service. Mike was a pilot with Affret-Air, a job which was deemed 'essential services' and excused him from military service. When he could find the time, he flew with the Police Reserve Air Wing (PRAW), ferrying senior officers and occasionally being called on to support ground troops. Pip was farming at Centenary, in the North East of the country. He was commissioned into 2nd Battalion The Rhodesian Regiment (2RR) and later transferred to his local PATU. Dillo, who was helping Nigel to farm Merryhill, was in the 3rd Battalion The Rhodesian Regiment (3RR) and then in Farm Watch, a different kind of local quick reaction force.

Richard also began the war as a farm manager in Centenary and was in the 2nd Battalion (2RR) and then a PATU. Nigel understood the pressures they were under only too well and explained to Robin in South Africa in December 1979 that *"It's not comforting killing and being shot at one day & trying to concentrate on an exacting civilian job the next, to say nothing of the responsibilities of command"*.

As the farms started to come under attack, security fences were put up to keep intruders out and then blast walls, designed to minimise the effects of mortar rounds. A system of radio alarms was installed, working to a permanently manned central control, and farmers organised themselves into a fighting guard force that could respond quickly, often on motorcycles, to a call for help from a neighbouring farm under attack. The first time Nigel was called out, he handed Corona a gun with the instruction to shoot to kill, before disappearing.

She, not knowing what else to do, quietly went to bed. Mines were a constant hazard, particularly on dirt roads where they could more easily be buried. One Wedza farmer had nine farm workers killed by a single mine attack.

Nigel wrote to a friend in England during a brief lull in the fighting in 1975 that *"Rhodesia today, except round the fringes, is probably as peaceful, happy and law abiding a country as any in the world. There are a thousand or so terrorists in and around our borders.... but I'm utterly confident that we can cope very effectively with anything the black states, even with Russian and Chinese arms and training, can throw against us."*

By 1978 he was sounding less optimistic. *"Quite apart from attacks on white homesteads – we've had four on neighbours this past month, during two of which we could actually hear the heavy stuff going off – they've developed a possibly even more worrying technique recently of attacking and burning farm compounds with odd murders and mutilations – castrating males, cutting the lips off women – which of course drives all the labour into the high hills. I may say that these animals are the followers of one Robert Mugabe ...we're not beaten yet, by a long chalk, but we're all living under a bit of a strain, as you may imagine."*

Things got very tense towards the end. Farmers and farm workers were being shot at and vehicles ambushed. All the farmers carried weapons with them everywhere, keeping a loaded rifle in the dining room and another by their beds. No-one went out at night when the gates in the security fences were locked and dogs released to patrol the grounds inside. From time to time they would meet at the Club, in the daylight of early afternoon, open up the bar and relax with a drink in the company of friends. It was a very necessary release of tension.

Merryhill was never attacked, although Pip's farm at Centenary was, while his wife and two young sons were alone in the house. There was, however, a famous occasion on which Nigel was ambushed. He had been to an ICA meeting at the Club and had had several drinks afterwards before setting out for home as dusk fell.

He decided to drive back round by the Numwa road rather than going straight across the farm since there were some newly laid irrigation pipes on the farm roads that he did not want to have to negotiate.

He was ambushed from the side of the road just beyond the Numwa barns. Luckily, as is often the case with inexperienced troops, the fire was high and did no harm to Nigel or the vehicle. In fact, he initially thought that his rattletrap of a Renault had developed some expensive sounding new noises, until he recognised the tracer flying past his windscreen. His first reaction was to return fire but, while looking down and struggling to extricate his rifle from under the seat, he travelled a hundred yards, crossed another road and put his car into the ditch, his lights pointing up into the sky at an angle of 45 degrees. Luckily, by then he was beyond the ambush zone. Having got hold of his rifle, he sat there for a while to get his bearings and then, aware that he only had four rounds with him, he extricated himself from the ditch and drove on to Richard's house.

Richard had heard the shooting, informed the police and called out his PATU 'stick' by radio, nominating a rendezvous at a neighbour's barn. The four-man 'stick', typically with a minimum of three 7.62 mm FN rifles and a 7.62 mm medium automatic gun (MAG) in support, was the basic tactical unit of both Army and Police. Richard's 'stick' did not cover itself with glory on this occasion. Half of them turned out from the bar at the Club in a condition in which they were going to be of little use to Richard. They ignored the rendezvous and set up a stop group of their own on the road that had been ambushed. They argued so fiercely about where to site it that two stormed off home and the rest promptly fell asleep on the roadside. Richard had been interrupted in his preparations by the arrival of Nigel, hoping for a much-needed drink. Only when Richard excused himself because he had to investigate an ambush did Nigel rather sheepishly confess that he had been the target.

Meanwhile, Johnny Travers, son of Nigel's friend and neighbour Norman Travers, having heard the shooting and seen Nigel's headlights pointing into the sky, decided not to wait for the rest of the 'stick' and persuaded his father to drive him to the ambush site in a borrowed truck. They came under fire and Johnny, standing in the back of the truck with his back against the cab and his machine gun slung over his shoulder, returned it enthusiastically. Unfortunately he clipped the corner of the cab, leaving a neat row of bullet holes just behind his father's head. At that short range the metal of the cab stripped the jackets from the bullets, which flew round the cab like a swarm of bees.

The final event in this comedy of errors came while Richard was on the radio telling the police that he could hear a second ambush. He was interrupted by the excited voice of Johnny's girlfriend, later his wife, who was spending a clandestine night with him, telling him that it was Johnny and Norman who were under fire. The girl's mother, listening in to see if she could help, heard and recognised her voice and interrupted the radio conversation with an aghast and undeniable *"Is that you, Judy?"*

Richard took over from Dillo at Merryhill in 1978. The idea was for Nigel to hand over the tobacco and go on looking after his beloved Herefords. However, he found it hard to let go and defining the boundaries needed careful handling by both Dillo and Richard, until Nigel came to see that his sons' energy, hard work and appetite for innovations that sometimes alarmed him were paying off. When Richard went over to Europe in 1983, Nigel took back the farm temporarily and found it hard work, getting tired and frustrated and letting things worry him much more than they used to. He told Robin that *"I shall be glad to see him back... though I've been rather thrilled to be in the saddle again. Also*

I've built another dam... I shall probably get a rocket for wasting diesel but I've had my fun. To be named Grandpa's Folly." By 1985 he was ready to hand over even the cattle.

The war had been brought to an end in December 1979, when Britain and Rhodesia's African neighbours ran out of patience. Elections followed in February 1980 and Robert Mugabe became Premier of an independent Zimbabwe in April 1980. At first, many whites were prepared to give him a chance. When he visited Marandellas in February 1985, Nigel felt that, right or wrong, he was at least sincere. As it turned out, he was only accepting the support of white farmers until he felt secure. Then he turned on them, not least because he had to appease the thousands of ex-guerrillas who thought they had been fighting for land.

'War veterans' arrived on Merryhill in 2000, after Nigel's death, in the wake of a notice from the Government that gave Corona, Richard and his family ninety days to get off the farm. The new arrivals set up camp on Sheffield, on the opposite side of the dam to Corona's house. They built huts, cut down the 'msasa' trees for firewood and brought in cattle. They forced the farm workers to attend compulsory all night meetings for 're-education' and Richard had to negotiate with them every time he needed to plough one of the tobacco lands to which they laid claim or if his cattle ate 'their' mealies. Nigel's gum plantations were cut down and the wood sold - some of it by the Wedza District Administrator. Cattle were hamstrung and butchered for meat. Snares were set for game and the dams netted for fish. Corona wrote *"I am so thankful that Nigel did not have to see the devastation of all he built up"* and that feeling of relief was echoed repeatedly by his family.

A year later, at the age of ninety one, Corona was attacked in her own house by four intruders. She was struck by a stone from a catapult, robbed, amongst other things, of the .410 shotgun that her father had given her, and left unconscious on the floor of her bedroom. She then walked, half naked and without a stick, the mile and a half to Richard's house. Once there she calmly said *"I think I am going into shock. Please make me some tea and get a blanket"*. They made her comfortable on the sofa and sent for an ambulance. While she was on the sofa, covered with a blanket and drinking sweet tea and whisky, a seven foot long python appeared on the window sill behind her. Even at that grim moment, the extraordinary incongruity of the encounter made her laugh and restored some perspective to the whole incident for her.

She moved into a cottage within sound of Richard's house for another year but the increasingly violent campaign by the 'war veterans', which she always regarded as the fourth war through which she had lived, eventually became too much. In the run-up to the 2002 election Richard and Gilly persuaded her to go and stay with Pip in Mozambique.

An air force veteran named Munyaradzi had moved into the tobacco barns from where he was able to control the farm workers' compound and the cattle, making free use of a .303 rifle in both endeavours. When Richard heard that it was him, not Munyaradzi, whom the police were seeking to arrest, he decided that they had to leave. They packed up, cursing the huge family portraits that Nigel and Corona had brought out from England. The farm staff moved into the house behind the security fence where they felt safer. Richard could obviously not go back, so his wife Gilly rode over with Jeffery, who helped her to look after the horses, at four o'clock one morning to drive off the four dairy cows and five horses. Twice they had to hide the beasts from Munyaradzi, who was driving up and down the roads, looking for Richard, but they eventually got them the twenty five kilometres to the Agricultural College, to which they presented them at the end of a long, emotional and physically exhausting day.

After more than fifty years, Merryhill had been stolen.

CHAPTER 10
JOURNEYS AND HOMECOMINGS

Corona was always interested in archaeology. In 1978, when Nigel wanted to go back to England to shoot a goose again, they agreed that Corona should take herself off to somewhere she really wanted to go. She had just been reading about Machu Picchu, the pre-Columbian Inca site in Peru, and the Mayan temple of Tikal in Guatemala. She also wanted to see her sister Rose, then living in a convent on St Lucia. She flew from Johannesburg to Lima, taking the wise traveller's precaution of reinforcing the handles of her handbag with metal tigerfish trace to prevent them from being cut. From Lima she went by bus and train to Cuzco, a three day trip into the mountains. With companions she had met on the way, she got up early to make the hour and a half climb to Machu Picchu, five square miles of temples, palaces and public buildings on steep hillsides connected by three thousand steps, beating not only the sun, but also the tourists.

In Guatemala, everyone seemed to her to be helpful and friendly. She found places to eat and to stay and hired a canoe to take her across the lagoons to the temple at Tikal. On the way back to Guatemala City, her bus broke down on the road. Unperturbed, she hitched a lift in a cattle lorry. It did not do her back much good, which was painful for the rest of the trip, but she travelled on to stay with Rose in her Benedictine mission on St Lucia. On the way home, Corona managed to get on the wrong bus and miss her plane. She spent the night on a bench in the airport and had to talk her way onto a different plane in the morning. She was then sixty seven years old.

Closer to home, she became interested in the granite koppies that dot the area around Wedza Mountain. They had been much used over the centuries as places of refuge, firstly by the Bushmen, who left their distinctive paintings, and later by Shona tribes hiding from Matabele raiding parties. Corona undertook a course at the Salisbury Museum and was then tasked by them to find, and trace for their records, Bushmen paintings throughout the Wedza tribal lands. At first, she painted them in their original colours but archaeological practice came to prefer black outlines only, on the grounds that the colours would have changed over the years. Although the boys used to refer to her half scale reproductions rather disparagingly as *"Mum's comic strips"*, they are beautifully done and many are still displayed in the Zimbabwe National Art Gallery.

She was introduced to archaeologist Sheila Rudd by friends and assisted her to excavate the Tsindi ruins. Professor Tom Huffman of the Salisbury Museum was also an early inspiration. She accompanied him on a major dig at Great Zimbabwe. Being used to Merryhill, she was better able than some of her companions to cope with the spiders and insect life in the temporary long-drop loos but she never learnt to accept the sociability of having three seats side by side behind the reed screens. She simply got up earlier and earlier each morning in the quest for privacy.

After ten days of instruction under Professor Huffman, she was granted a permit to conduct a dig of her own on a neighbour's farm at Wedza where irregular heaps of stones were thought to indicate burial sites. Corona carefully recorded the way the stones were arranged, before removing them, layer by successive layer. She was thrilled to discover a skeleton belonging to a Shona woman, lying on her side with her knees drawn up and with two deliberately broken pots by her side.

She then obtained a permit to dig for pottery on Castle Kopje on Norman Travers' farm at Imire. She chose a site that she thought looked interesting and cleared the ground at the entrance to a cave-like structure between two towering granite columns. Two African helpers dug down, inch by inch, while Corona sieved every particle of soil they dug up. About eighteen inches down, she found a hut floor made of baked mud and dung. This was removed and after a month, when they had got down about three feet, she uncovered an unmistakably gold bracelet that looked as fresh as though it was displayed on a jeweller's counter. Quickly emptying a bucket of earth over it to hide it, she raced home and rang the Museum to report the discovery of a 'gold burial'. Inevitably, the conduct of the dig was taken over by others but it turned out to be an important find, carbon-dated to 1450 AD, of a Great Zimbabwean. There was more gold in the form of arm and leg bangles and hair decorations. Some of the pottery was even older, being carbon-dated to 1260-1280 AD. The finds are all now in the National Museum in Harare, although they are not credited to Corona, an amateur and a white woman.

The Castle Kopje find was important enough for her to be invited to talk on it to The Pre-History Society in Salisbury and various other learned bodies of what Nigel, despite his immense pride in her achievements, persisted in calling *"archaeowobblers"*. He reported to Robin *"Ma doing splendid things with her dig on Castle Kopje and has all the fundis (experts) at the Museum gasping with admiration and green with envy as apparently she has unearthed a type of pottery of far earlier origins than normal."* For her first talk, in Salisbury, she created a set of beautiful drawings to be projected onto a screen with which to illustrate it. She wore a scarlet embroidered Mandarin-style coat to boost her confidence for the talk, which she later wore for their fiftieth wedding anniversary.

She subsequently corresponded with, and was visited on the farm by, the international rock art expert David Coulson, Founder and Chairman of the Trust for African Rock Art (TARA) and co-author with Alec Campbell of the definitive book 'African Rock Art'. She took them to see a remarkable site she had discovered with a life-sized painting of a human figure which looked like a skeleton. Above it were figures with distended abdomens, normally regarded as suggesting trance or an out of body experience. Corona, from her extensive knowledge

 of other sites, was able to point to similarities with a painting at Diana's Vow near Rusape. Her theories impressed David Coulson sufficiently for him to want to publish them.

She became well-known and highly regarded in Zimbabwe, although as an amateur she had to tread carefully to avoid becoming entangled in professional rivalries. She was invited to conferences in Namibia and South Africa and eventually to speak at one in Australia. She wanted to read for a degree in Archaeology but discovered that she needed to have an Anthropology degree first. She took a two year Diploma on Biblical Archaeology instead. She did not find it easy to write about pottery of types she had never handled from sites she had never seen, but at least, she said, she had Nigel's help in correcting her English.

Her work often took her to isolated areas on her own, scrambling up and down the koppies with the aid of a light ladder which Pip made for her from bamboo and without apparent regard for the dangers from guerrillas or from wild animals. There is a famous story of how she hid herself in the hole she was excavating, while a clearly rabid jackal walked past about ten yards away, before going back to the farmhouse to get a gun.

In 1986 Corona had enough money coming in from the picture business to take a trip to see the Great Wall of China and the Terracotta Army, thousands of life-sized statues of warriors that had been discovered there in 1974. It moved her to tears and she described it as *"one of the great wonders of the world"*. Nigel was not in the least interested and stayed in England with his brother Guy in Shropshire, doing some shooting and fishing, and visiting Peter Scott's Wildfowl Trust at Slimbridge. Nevertheless he missed her and wrote to Robin that *"It's going to be pure heaven seeing her again."*

The following year Corona visited Egypt, impressing her guide on a camel ride out to the pyramids by disdaining the stirrups and riding in the correct position with crossed feet. She went on a painting course in Italy and visited Rome on her way home, describing the Coliseum as *"redolent of wild beasts and death"*, but finding the ceiling of the Sistine chapel *"indescribably magnificent"*. While she was in Italy she made friends with an American, Ted Sanuella, who came out to Zimbabwe to stay at Merryhill and whom she saw again in Moscow when she did a Russian trip. She made another good friend there, Tina Wheeler, an American with whom she subsequently stayed in London.

Because of her reputation as an authority on Bushmen paintings, Corona was invited to deliver a paper at a Rock Art Congress in Darwin, Australia in 1988, a remarkable achievement for a seventy seven year old amateur. Nigel was not well and went down to South Africa to stay with Dillo and his family while she was away. After the conference, many of the delegates hired cars and camping equipment and went to look at rock art in the Kakadu National Park. There were about a hundred people in the group, which was too many to organise easily. Expeditions started late and ran on into the hottest part of the day but they saw some interesting paintings, quite different from the African ones. On the third day she was called back from halfway up a mountain to take a telephone call at Park Headquarters, about an hour's drive away. It was, as she feared, from Richard to say that Nigel had died in Pietermaritzburg Hospital on 4th September 1988.

Corona took herself off for a walk and, in her words, *"sobbed and bellowed and wailed"* until she had got all the sadness out and could face the rest of the party without a tear. She and Nigel had already agreed that she would not rush back if the worst happened and she went on with her trip, although she confessed that she lost some of her enthusiasm for rock paintings and skipped several of the planned visits, preferring a boat trip along the Yellow River, watching hundreds of magpie geese and whistling duck.

Nigel was flown back to Harare and is buried in the garden of the new house, looking out over Scott's Dam. All five of his sons and his sister Puss, who was flown out from England by Mike, were there. The grave is not marked, except by a 'msasa' tree.

105

Corona came home to the empty house by the dam that they had planned for their retirement. She removed Nigel's study so that the hall ran right through the house from the front door to the French windows that looked into the garden. Josephine, her maid, became more of a companion than a maid and neither of them paid much regard to the dust that gathered in the house.

Corona lived a pretty full life there, painting and sketching, fishing, learning French, doing a course on how to identify trees, writing up her life story on an old typewriter and getting to know her grandchildren, Richard's children, who lived at the other end of the dam. She watched cricket, played the organ in church, gave talks on rock art, played bridge every week either at Merryhill or on a neighbour's farm and learnt aerobics. The rose garden at the new house became as notable as the one at the old, and there were always bowls of roses or of wild flowers in the house. Corona won a prize or two at flower shows despite fierce competition.

At her 80th birthday party she made a memorable speech in which she thanked her five sons for the gift of ten daughters-in-law between them, with most of whom she managed to remain friends. Visits and visitors were frequent and important to her, not least from her sons and their families. She remained independent, spurning help when scrambling up and down steep koppies at what others might have regarded as an advanced age. On a visit to Dillo and his family in South Africa, despite having two artificial hips, she rode again, cantering at the age of eighty two, and loved it. She was still driving at ninety, almost blind, with Jonah, her gardener, beside her to tell her if a car was coming the other way.

When she was no longer able to live at Merryhill because of the threat from 'war veterans', she moved to Casa Msika in Mozambique to join Pip where he was running a holiday and fishing camp. By a happy coincidence, he already had her old canoe there, which she took over again. She set out to make herself useful, inspecting the rooms every day and busying herself in the kitchens, to Pip's consternation, but earning the awed respect of the Mozambican staff. She began to learn Portuguese. Practical as ever, when she needed a feather duster to deal with spiders' webs, she simply plucked a couple of feathers from one of the ostriches Pip was farming. She still did her daily walk and it was at Casa Msika that she sat down to rest with her back against a log, which turned out to have harboured a nest of pepper ticks. When she returned to the house she complained of an itchy back and wondered if she was allergic to the prawns she ate almost daily. She had to have an astonishing 385 pepper ticks removed from her back with a pair of tweezers.

Tragically, Pip died in May 2003 and after burying him at Casa Msika, Corona returned to Zimbabwe. In the end she buried not only her husband but three of her sons and a grand-daughter. Robin and his daughter Kate had died in a microlight accident in Durban, South Africa, in September 1991. Mike was killed in a plane accident in Halifax, Canada, in October 2004. Just as after Nigel's death, there were those who expressed astonishment, and sometimes disapproval, at her extraordinary resilience in the face of tragedy, perhaps making the mistake of assuming that, because she did not show her feelings, she did not have any. Unlike Nigel, she simply did not express her emotions easily or publicly. She had an enormous inner strength and a reserve that could give her a regal, rather distant air. She actively encouraged the myth that she never cried, but those who knew her best knew that was not true.

Richard and Gilly found her a retirement home at Borradaile, but she was extremely reluctant to go, saying that she was not ready for what she called *"the departure lounge"*. In the end she accepted that it made sense and then, as was her habit, made the best of the situation, comparing it to going back to boarding school. She was delighted to find her friends the Travers already installed there and looked forward to the regular parcels from Ted Sanuella in America, containing cheese, coffee and sardines and CDs and tapes of opera and audio books which she loved. The family had a lot of trouble in persuading Ted not to write the full value of the contents on the label so that they did not have to pay excessive amounts of duty.

She continued to believe that it was really only acceptable to sit down and relax after lunch. She drew or painted every morning right up to the end, despite her failing sight. Unable to see small canvasses, she created a Mozambican scene across her white cupboard doors in black felt tip pen that she was constantly adding to. She helped out in the second hand shop and walked twice a day. Even when her sight was all but gone, an offer of a guiding arm was likely to be summarily rejected.

Then she had an accident, falling into a bath of scalding hot water and burning herself badly. She amazed the doctors by her resilience but she died from the trauma on 30th May 2007. Because the 'war veterans' would not allow her back onto Merryhill, and there were no refrigeration or cremation facilities in Harare, she was buried quickly and quietly on a neighbour's farm, from where she could look out over a small dam with water lilies, wildfowl and other birds to her beloved Merryhill, with Wedza Mountain in the distance.